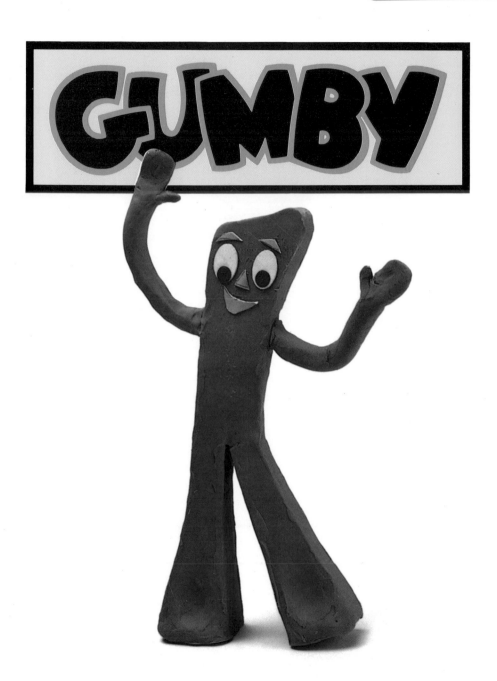

The Authorized Biography
of the World's Favorite Clayboy

GUMBY

by Louis Kaplan and Scott Michaelsen
in harmony with Art Clokey

HARMONY BOOKS
New York

Design by Janet Tingey
Manufactured in Japan

Library of Congress Cataloging-in-Publication Data

Kaplan, Louis.
Gumby: the authorized biography of the world's
favorite clayboy.
1. Adventures of Gumby (Television program)
2. Gumby (Fictitious character) I. Michaelsen, Scott.
II. Clokey, Art. III. Title.
PN1992.77.A26K37 1986 791.45′72 86-14862
ISBN 0-517-56266-9 (pbk.)
10 9 8 7 6 5 4 3 2
First Edition

For four pals

Contents

Foreword

BY ART CLOKEY

Gumby was a by-product of an art film I made in 1953, called *Gumbasia*. In *Gumbasia,* I filmed geometric and amorphous shapes made from modeling clay of many colors. These shapes moved and transformed to the background rhythm of jazz.

I wanted to avoid as much as possible the distraction of any recognizable forms in *Gumbasia*. It was an experiment in pure movement, where the whole plane moved out in different shapes this way and that. *Gumbasia* was filled with movements that, when put together, created a feeling. For instance, there was a shot showing a ball rolling through clay arches and the next shot showed the ball going over a little hill. You begin to *feel* the movement. In the early 1970s,

Gumbasia. *Geometric and amorphous shapes moved and transformed.*

Playboy used that scene in a feature called "Sex in Cinema." (I could never understand why.)

Sam Engel, a major movie producer, had asked to see my film. I had met Sam because, at that time, I was tutoring his son in English and Latin at Harvard Military Academy (now Harvard School) in Los Angeles. "This is the most exciting film I have ever seen in my life!" Sam said. When Sam comments that a film is exciting, God listens; otherwise He might miss out on something big!

We immediately formed a partnership. Sam had just finished a film starring Burt Lancaster and Sophia Loren, and my repressed libido was turning out fantasies of helping to direct Sam's next picture, with Sophia, Marilyn Monroe, or Jayne Mansfield. I soon learned, however, that I would turn in my libido for a box of clay. Since Sam had another son who was about three years old, he was interested in the quality of children's fare on television. He could see that my trimensional animation process would be perfect for children's films. Imagine my disappointment at his suggestion that I work on a clay figure instead of Sophia's!

I trudged home to do my asexual as-signment, never having dreamed that I would be involved in making movies for children—prepubescent children at that! For weeks I played around with clay—molding many shapes and colors, looking for the right figure. Although it could never compare with the "casting couch" routine, tabletop modeling became a fascinating challenge to my imagination.

Clay is the basic medium for creative conception of new forms. It's malleable and it changes every time you touch it. You push and mash it, and a lump turns into something, just like magic.

I set out to create a shape and size that were functionally practical from the film animating standpoint. Animating clay for hours under hot lights created a problem: I found it necessary to have a shape and size that were easily reproduced, so that a fresh figure could be substituted as the old one became dirty and completely misshapen through excessive manipulation.

Part of the idea behind *Gumbasia* was that everything in life is based on geometric forms. Gumby and Pokey are close to that. They are simple forms and combinations of those forms. If you roll some white clay into a ball, slit it in half, and place each on a side of Pokey's head, you have his eyes. And when Pokey's eyes bug out, they come out as rods.

Gumby's shape is simple but I didn't want him to become a phallic symbol. We put a little bump on his head to give him the bump of wisdom that the Buddhists have. The only difference is that they have it in the center and Gumby's is over to the side. Actually, the real inspiration for this bump came from my early childhood. In the living room of my grandfather's farmhouse in Michigan hung a framed photo enlargement of my father, taken when he was eighteen. It showed a cowlick on one side of his head that looked like a large bump. I was so amazed by it.

Early Gumby and Pokey models. I found it necessary to have a shape and size that were easily reproduced.

Arthur Farrington, Art Clokey's father. We put a little bump on his head to give him the bump of wisdom.

If you superimpose an outline of that portrait over Gumby, you will see that the heads coincide perfectly.

As for size, I finally settled on a seven-inch Gumby, as this turned out to be the easiest to work with. Rolling out a large slab of half-inch-thick clay, I was able to create a number of Gumby bodies in a few minutes with a homemade "cookie cutter." The arms were rolled separately and cut from lengths of long snakelike pieces of clay. Soft wire was inserted into both the arms and the body to give needed rigidity. The eyes were little disks of white clay, cut and bent for various expression changes, and the pupils were tiny balls of red clay that stuck to the white disks. These balls were easily rolled about to create a variety of expressions. The eyebrows, mouth, and nose were made of yellow stringlike pieces that stuck to the green body.

Green with a hint of blue was what I chose for Gumby's color. Imagine a luxuriant field on a bright day when the green

The Zoops. *I developed no formulas.*

grass picks up just a pinch of blue sky. Gumby looks like a fat blade of grass. I am sure Walt Whitman would have been pleased. Pokey, on the other hand, is all earth—orange and black. Pokey is skeptical and down to earth, as opposed to Gumby, who has both feet on the ground but his head in the clouds.

As for Gumby's name, I had learned the term "gumbo" as a child in Michigan. During the rainy season, before they had pavement through the farm country, the roads got very slippery and mucky. My father would come home and tell us that he had "gotten stuck in the gumbo" on the farm. From my years of studying Latin,

I knew that the diminutive of "gumbo" is a "Gumbino" or "Gumby," and the mother was "Gumba," which is the female declension in Latin. "Gumbo" is the masculine. Seven years of the language and that's the only way I ever used it.

Later, I created the characters of Prickle and Goo, who were inspired by my association and friendship with Alan Watts. One day he said rather humorously that there are two kinds of people in the world, the prickly and the gooey. The prickly are the rigid and uptight, and the gooey are the easygoing and flowing. I then decided to make two characters who symbolized these two types. One was a spiked dino-

Art Clokey and friends. The strongest thing I ever took was coffee or orange juice.

saur, called Prickle, and the other was a little blue mermaid named Goo. The female is more gooey and the male is prickly. (Please keep your chuckles clean.)

I took the Gumby pilot to Tom Sarnoff at NBC, who was immediately charmed by the character and by the style of clay animation. He signed me to produce a series of *The Adventures of Gumby*. Roger Muir, the producer of *Howdy Doody*, agreed after seeing the film that it would be a winner, and decided to introduce Gumby on his show. Gumby then graduated to his own show, *The Gumby Show*, with Pinky Lee as the emcee. Pinky Lee may have chafed under that title; I think

he resented playing second fiddle to a piece of clay.

NBC gave me complete artistic freedom, which is something almost unheard of now at a network. I would just fantasize and daydream. Some of the people I meet today say that I must have "taken something" to do all those surrealistic things in Gumby. I have to tell them that I never did. I never smoked marijuana or took psychedelics while making the films. I was very afraid of drugs all my life. I didn't know anything about them. The strongest thing I ever took was coffee or orange juice.

Sometimes I would tell my children bedtime stories and turn them into Gumbys. I developed no formulas. Each episode was a separate creation. I never knew what the next episode was going to be about. The love I had for my children rubbed off on those stories. I was just enjoying creating.

I think one of the reasons for Gumby's appeal is that it has the spirit of love—for my children and for children of any age. Kids like Gumby because all the details aren't filled in for them. Gumby is more sensuous than cell-animated cartoon characters because he appeals to more senses than cartoon characters do. Kids can put themselves into it and imagine all kinds of

The Fantastic Farmer. *He might get smashed but he always comes back.*

things with Gumby. They are fascinated by this simple gingerbread-man-like figure who could do almost anything.

The most recent resurgence in Gumby's popularity started in 1979, when my wife, Gloria, and I went to India to see avatar Sathya Sai Baba. Sai Baba can materialize objects out of thin air; you can't believe it unless you see it. Strings of beads and gold rings just come out of his hand. I stood there with Gumby and he did this circular motion with his arms. I could see the sacred ash coming out of his hand. He plopped it right on Gumby, and when we came home things started to happen. The episodes started appearing on TV again, sales of the Gumby toys began to pick up, and then Eddie Murphy did his Gumby skit on *Saturday Night Live.* My son Joe came to me and asked why I let Eddie Murphy do that to Gumby. I told him that

you have to understand humor. Gumby has to laugh at himself too. Gumby is a symbol of the spark of divinity in each of us, the basis of the ultimate value of each person. Eddie Murphy instinctively picked up on this when he asserted, "I'm Gumby, dammit!" When people watch *The Adventures of Gumby* today, they get a blissful feeling. After years of being grown up and crushed by life's downers, we yearn again for that Gumby high.

And how does Gumby feel about his renewed popularity? Well, he really doesn't have a reaction; he accepts it. He says that everybody is unusual and exciting and interesting, and everybody is like him. There's no situation Gumby can't handle. He might get smashed, but he always comes back.

Gumby loves you. We love you. That's about all I can say.

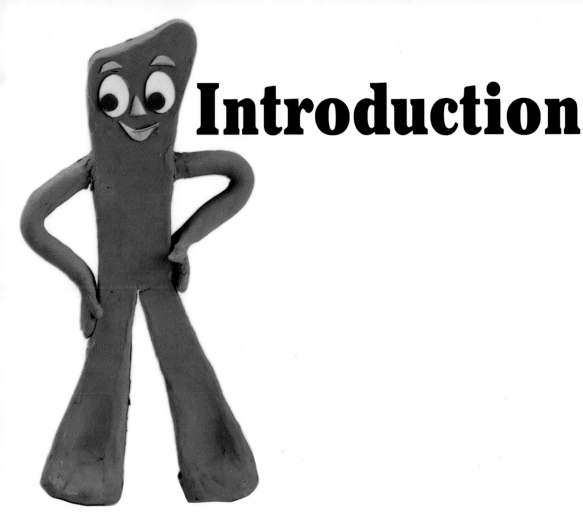

Introduction

Gumby led them on.

Scott pushed through the aisle of the video store. Before his eyes, a copy of *Gumby Adventure #1* appeared. At another time and in another place, he found himself holding copies of *Gumby's Incredible Journey* and *Gumby's Holiday Adventure*. Over and over he watched the episodes **The Fantastic Farmer, Too Loo,** and **Santa Witch,** mesmerized by clay in motion.

Meanwhile, Louis was busy moving into a new apartment. He had a sense of euphoria here. Two weeks later, fumbling in the hallway for his keys, he noticed at eye level a slightly raised surface. A four-inch-high image, an impression left in a residue of glue—Gumby. His apartment had been visited.

They had visions of a book, but spreading the word was no easy matter. A chosen few thought they were trying to form a religious cult. Some read the first words—on Gumby alchemy—and frowned. But Gumby would not be stopped, and a pact with Harmony Books (whose interest in matters spiritual dates back to the publication of its first title, *Be Here Now* by Ram Dass) soon followed.

Before long, Louis and Scott were flying to California to connect with Gumby film makers Art and Gloria Clokey. The magic transmissions increased tenfold. Art had arranged for the two acolytes to lodge with a group of modern-day alchemists at the Elysium Institute in Topanga. Much was laid bare. The two were later drawn, along with Harmony's Owen O'Donnell, to a wonderful dinner at the Inn of the Seventh Ray, yet another magical place. Their waitress looked deep into their hearts and told them that they too were alchemists. Synchronicities continued to multiply. Art, Gloria, Scott, and Louis celebrated their good fortune with a bottle of Carl Jung rosé wine at the Golden Temple. Louis later claimed that he felt a lump growing on his forehead—the Gumby bump of wisdom.

The words came quickly. Within months, *Gumby* was born. They had lived the meaning of a message: "If you've got a heart, then Gumby is a part of you." Louis and Scott had been the instrument of clay consciousness, called to become Gumby's ghostwriters.

The book passed on, through publication, into the hands of all, writing itself onto those who opened it.

Cast of Characters

Gumby—a clayboy

Pokey—Gumby's pony pal

Prickle—a miniature dinosaur friend of Gumby and Pokey

Goo—the blue claygirl who rounds out the quartet of best playmates

The Blockheads—Gumby's adversaries, with "G" and "J" alphabet blocks for heads

Gumbo and Gumba—Gumby's dad and mom

Professor Kap—Gumby's experimenting scientist mentor

Nopey—Gumby's dog who'll only give "no" for an answer

The Groobee—Gumby's beelike pet that carries a hammer and builds boxes

King Ott—the ruler of the medieval storybook kingdom of Roo

The Black Knight—a nemesis who threatens the kingdom of Roo

Henry and Rodgy—a brown bear and his sculpted friend who share a separate series of adventures

The Pesky Indians—a tribe led by Chief Running Bear; sometimes they're allies, othertimes troublemakers

Farmer Glenn—the farmer who raised Pokey and lives in the book *Western Stories*

Dr. Zveegee—a mad scientist bent on ruining the claymates' fun

Richard the Lion—an adventurous pal who lives at the zoo

Gumby Clayboy

Gumbo

He was once a little green slab of clay. You should see what Gumby can do today. Let's see or, better yet, feel things out—touch on the tactile. This boy's famous shape: up top, his eraserhead—a lump, a bumpy bit, a top that just won't balance. Then a pair of mitts and two stubby stems indented inward. With everything gone green. That's about it for this body without organs. All of which makes Gumby pretty neat, even elementary.

He's a simple clayboy, living with a storybook Mom and Dad, Gumbo and Gumba. Sharing adventures with a pal named Pokey—a, well, red horse hailing from a volume called *Western Stories*. His closest companions include the world's only living dinosaur, Prickle, and the plump, blue, girlish Goo.

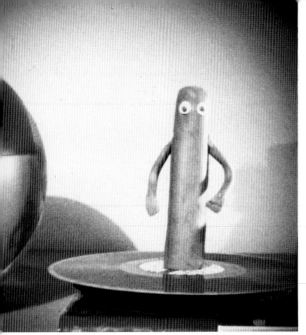

Lion Drive. *A spin on a turntable turns him into a record-length rod.*

Who's What? *I just pounded it together like this, and put that on that.*

But who? Gumby's name is mud. He's "gumbo," a kind of sticky soil. Something you can really get your hands in and rub up against. Something you can pile up as patties or smush flat as a flapjack. Gumby is an everymud, an example of infinite malleability. Whatever size the slot, Gumby fits. Any way you slice him he comes up gum.

Carve through Gumby and outline some clay configurations. Loads of cases: sliding through a truck door, plopping to a clay puddle, skyscraping against a building wall. A spin on a turntable turns him into a record-length rod in **Lion Drive.** He wrings dry like a dishrag during **Toy Joy.** And in **G.F.D. (Gumby Fire Department),** Gumby, Pokey, and Prickle drop down a fire pole and smash to one multicolor mass.

Carloads of cases. In **Gumby Racer,** the boys' sports coupe grinds to a halt. Looks like Gumby's out of the race, but Dad reminds Gumby that he's a mean green machine. In the clutch Gumby handles the matter, hands down. He turns the keys on the Gumby-mobile—a pretty swift switch from green guy to rolling racer. An actual earthmover. Dad gets revved up: "Now you're going to see a real race." The clayboy is taking a crack and a whack, and this wacky Gumby-mobile takes on everyone and everything. Getting ahead by splitting down the middle, moving straight through other cars, even sinking below gumbo. By the time they reach the finish line, Gumby and Pokey have changed the course of the race.

In **Who's What?,** Gumby's first cousin Henry sets aside time for clay. Henry is bored with "Stuffy old dolls, old stuffed rags." Stuffy is much too stiff. He likes mucking around with clay. The raw material that matters more. So he sculpts his very own claymate, Rodgy—an unknown quantity with peaked beak and big belly. Rodgy wants to be someone, in a finished mold. He wants to be pigeonholed. "I'm not just clay. I'm a bird," he posits. But Henry refuses to let the dust settle. "I just pounded it together like this, and put that on that. And then like this and so, and that's all. You're clay." But hey! "You are the sculptor? You molded me?" Rodgy whines, holding out for something to hold on to. "You're my master!" Henry huffs, "Phooey! You're clay." Chased by a lion, Rodgy runs around in circles, circling back to slime mold.

Who's what? Clay is the culprit: Rodgy is put back in his place, back to gumbo. The hot spot from which all Gumby adventure takes off. Clay's bursts, bubbles, and breaks can't be held back or controlled. And yet it's all shaping up quite nicely, thank you. A clay-off—and running. Off your marks. Get unset. Let 'er rip.

Mercurial Matters

Clayboys worry about the weather. It's just a question of temperature. The play of clay is shaped by degrees. Tempered.

Two forecasts: warm means elastic and fantastic—a nice day where anything can happen—but frigid makes for rigid, and that spells catastrophe.

So Gumby packs along a Gumbometer on his adventures, and keeps in touch with the semisolid state. Gumbometer bands: cold, cool, perfect, perfectly elastic. In **Little Lost Pony,** Mom advises her son to pack it up. "Put on your Gumbometer and make sure you get neither too hot nor too cold." And in **Toy Crazy** Gumby beds down with his Gumbometer by his side. Does Gumby dream of elastic sheep? The green guy models himself according to his birthday wishes, becoming guitar, airplane, xylophone. Dad notes, "His temperature's all right." The Gumbometer checks out perfectly elastic.

Little Lost Pony. *But frigid makes for rigid, and that spells catastrophe.*

But a cold front sets in and ice cream is its name. Gumby's rivals, the rock-hard Blockheads, crave the junk: visions of 100-ice-cream-cone-rewards dance in their heads in **Little Lost Pony.** And they use the sweet stuff to slow things down. Stuffing their faces in **Gumby Racer,** they flip it into Gumby's and Pokey's pusses.

While he would love some ice cream, Gumby has to watch his shape. In **The Blockheads,** Gumby orders up a chocolate milkshake without the ice cream. "It makes me so cold and stiff I can't move!" But the cool-as-ice Blockheads want to spoil his perfect figure. They slip Gumby a stiff drink—adding a scoop—and he's hard as a board. Gumby catches a cold. Overcast, he needs warm blankets and coffee to thaw out before bouncing back to give the Blockheads the last licking.

Temperature also figures in Gumby's many moon adventures. Again, the fear of cold haunts him. Pursued by the pyramidal bug-eyed moon monsters, Gumby drops into a crater, and the temperature drops too. Dad, in a fashionable fur coat, rushes to the rescue. Gumby moans, "It's so cold, I'm getting stiff. Hurry up, Dad." Dad brings the clayboy back to earth comatose, operating to fix Gumby's cold feet.

The weather report: better to break the ice than take an ice cream break. It's fair to say that a warm guy like Gumby thrives in a mild climate. To expand and contract, bend and stretch, stay in shape. An exercise in shape changing.

Goo

Goo is the one Gumby friend gummier than Gumby. Her name says it all: Goo means gooey. Most Gumby pals have suggestive shapes. You might guess that

The Blue Goo. *The Baron goes down from Goo in the face.*

Prickle's snout, tail, and fins detail a dino, and you'd be right. And Pokey is positively puppy and pony. But Goo's a glob. A blob.

Goo looks like a lump with a bump of a nose. Not a mammal but a primordial at work. A creature still about to be formed and formulated. Perhaps an amoeba or a protoplasm—so indefinite, amorphous. This virtuoso varies volume with virtual ease.

Sometimes the boys draw on her resources. Building a Tinker Toy tower in **The Reluctant Gargoyles,** Prickle uses Goo as an elevator. She loads up on rods at the first floor and stretches straight up to take them to the top. Later, in hot pursuit of the Blockheads, she puts space shipshape—forming a bridge over a passing train for Pokey's convertible.

All too often, though, she's a fifth wheel—the girl in the group, and a big bother for Gumby and the guys. Gumby's goofy business brainstorms—firefighting, private investigating, piano rolling—all include a job for Goo. She's the receptionist. And then when the action heats up, she's left behind! Gumby pooh-poohs, "No, Goo. It's a man's job. It's dangerous." But the battle of the sexes busts when

The Reluctant Gargoyles. *Thick-skulled numbskulls with children's building blocks for heads.*

danger nears. Gumby, Pokey, and Prickle's pedestrian ideas seek to solve, while Goo dissolves. Over and over she greets crisis with contour. The **Good Knight Story** tells the tale of Goo gluing a dragon's mouth shut while bungling Gumby stands by. After the boys destroy a fire engine and all its accouterments in **G.F.D. (Gumby Fire Department),** Goo thins into a safety net to catch a woozy Professor Kap and then stretches to tarp to cover the burning building. The Goo twist: turning outside-in.

As a ready-made ribbon and rubber band, she ties up the Blockheads in **The Ferris Wheel Mystery** and **Making Squares.** And in her finest hour, as **The Blue Goo,** she battles the Black Baron. A fine example of doing gooed. Taking off from the wing of Prickle's biplane, Goo transforms herself into a missile and bears down on the Baron. She spits clay bullets and engines sputter. The Baron goes down from goo in the face.

Goo is blue, it's true. She may be down,

but also up, across, and through. She slides along the surface and shifts in all dimensions all the time. Goo segments every second, manifolds every present moment of now. Wow.

The Blockheads—Hard Cases

Simply put, they're squares. Thick-skulled numbskulls with children's building blocks for heads and stupid smirks on faces. Letters "G" and "J," carved into their blocks to identify them, brand them. Time and again, a reluctant Gumby has to square off against the pesky Blockheads.

What makes them tick? The need to restrict, make normal. Unlike the clayboy, the straight-ahead and narrow-minded Blockheads are locked in, inflexible. The same old routine over and over again. Their **School for Squares** imposes a very rigid discipline indeed. Here, a little brick schoolhouse built to rebuild others—Indians—and replace teepee thinking with right-angled logic. Until Gumby comes and spins the blocks around, making them cone down for a change.

Making Squares—it's the same old scene for Pokey and Prickle. The Block-heads turn on the power and turn out assembly-line identicals. Goo's glum. "They're trying to make robots out of them." But Gumby takes over, putting the squareheads into round holes.

Blockheads breed roadblocks. Stopping stones. G and J will leave no stone unturned to slow the flow. A boulder blocks the way for **Gumby Racer.** Only a stopgap measure since the green guy slips right through the rocks. And blowing up bridg-es is in order because these squares can't stand to see anything spanning be-tween sides.

Slow-downs and jam-ups multiply. In **Even Steven,** they ditch Gumby and Pokey, sticking them in a rut like their own. They even log up and clog up the train tracks to topple the gang as part of their making-squares efforts. As if that wasn't enough blockage, the dim-witted dullards throw nets to tie things up even tighter.

Robots or gargoyles, these square clods plod along stiff and zombielike. Not sticky mud; sticks in the mud. While Gumby can walk into any book, G and J lack easy access, requiring a chain saw to carve out their niches in **Western Stories.** The goal in **All Broken Up** is to strike up the bland and put a stop to Goo's sculptural modeling, to get to the breaking point where nothing can be left to change. But in the end, right angles go wrong and the Blockheads crack under pressure. For all their schooling, G and J are much too thick to catch on to what clay's all about. A block, a rock, a stone that just won't roll. Becoming gets the better of a Block-head, with Gumby always a step ahead. Uncarving a lumphead— clay's way.

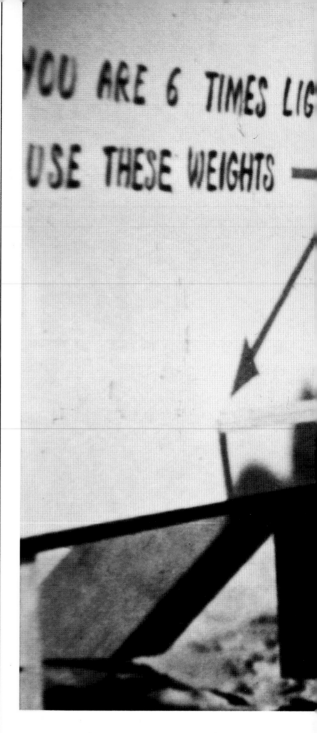

Whatever Became Of . . .

It's becoming obvious. Clayboys never grow old, never say die, never get out-molded. Even that famous face won't stay in place. Watch closely and see Gumby's huge forehead and big circle eyes in **Train Trouble,** among others. A scooped-out

Moon Trip. *Headlong changes in heading: no eyebrows, circle eyes, red pupils.*

mouth—with no outline—in **Even Steven.** Headlong changes in heading; clay variations. No eyebrows, yellow eyebrows, sculpted eyebrows. Circle eyes, oval eyes, red pupils, black pupils. Face the facts and size things up. Big Gumbys. Little Gumbys to ride toy cars and trains. Fat and thin Gumbys in **Mirrorland.**

Gumby greets, starts to converse: "Hi! I'm Gumby." But since he's a clayboy, he's already started to convert. Is no longer an "is." It's a hello that can be

Gumby Business #1 *(never aired). He may be bisected right down the middle.*

taken only in passing—never passing away. A young and very becoming clayboy like Gumby doesn't worry about such things, doesn't understand black humor. A smiling Gumby bares all before the **Black Knight** in a jousting match, while King Ott just can't bear to look. "This is going to be just awful. The Black Knight will slice Gumby to ribbons. Ohhh!" Another knight pronounces the death sentence: "No one who sees the Black Knight ever comes back alive." Even Pokey protests, "O.K. It's your funeral." But Gumby can't possibly lose his head. "A miracle! Gumby is still in one piece." Lances and armor may break, but Ott forgets that Gumby has no hang-ups about being bent, cut off, or cut up. He may be bisected right down the middle or rolled up into a ball, but this gumboy is not one to be chewed out or let rigor mortis set in.

The Black Knight may want to hold Gumby to a point or even rub him out, but the space of clay is spaced out. It involves a strange geometry. Plastic, perhaps even spastic. Spaces with shifting boundaries, curved air. As silly as putty.

Sleights of shape—a foxy box, a tricky ball, a puffball. Operations of a space to topple logic. A space to twist and turn over and over. **Foxy Box**—hardly bigger than a bread box, but stretching the limits of the imagination. Out come tractor, plow, and model airplane in quick succession. A cut to see inside the box and all of a sudden space has opened up and folded over. Plenty of room for Gumby to stand up and play engineer. Thrown out, it seems as if one Gumby size fits both sides. He winks—a closing and an opening.

The clayboy's way of the world. To be Gumby—or not to be. To be reborn again, forever green. Clay's play—re-creations. The shape of things to come, become.

Gumby Adventurer

Catch the Drift

Gumby is a first-class traveler. A jet-setter who just won't settle for less. Won't settle at all. He's a foreigner checking in to visit some mighty exotic sites; checking out some wild scenes. From the darkest jungles to the farthest planets. Adrift.

In flight. Surveying all the available maps won't help you follow Gumby's itinerary. He's booking passage with no reservations. Take an unchartered trip to uncharted **Hidden Valley.** Gumby fills up the car with some magic spring water and it takes off, up and away. Pokey looks nervous, but Gumby follows the drift: "Where's your spirit of adventure?"

For the stray-boy explorer, scheduled departures and arrivals fall by the runway-side. In **Northland Follies,** he's

Northland Follies. *Scheduled departures and arrivals fall by the runway-side.*

part of a travel package that's missed its destination. Gumby and Pokey are stowaways on an Air Force mail carrier. They wanted to wind up on the sunny beaches of Hawaii, but they got carried away. Beached all right. The mailbag drops amid Arctic drifts for a whirlwind tour.

With drift, the scene shifts. **How Not to Trap Lions** runs over the open range available to a drifter. Gumby and Pokey's car stalls out on a bridge somewhere in the wilds of Africa. When Gumby gets them going again, you can't believe your eyes. It looks like a cliff-hanger as the car power-drives up a steep mountain range. Steeper and steeper still until it's slanting straight up. But Gumby has not yet begun to reach his peak or make the grade. Scaling new heights of adventure and death-defying gravity, he's riding suspended, right-side wrong. Exploring every angle and putting himself into every

position within reach of the imagination.

Gumby goes every which way. Just so long as he's going, mobile. Living behind the wheel, on the road. Always straying . . . never staying in one place. "This is the life!" says Gumby during the cross-country road trip in **Even Steven.** In adventure, after adventure.

An exploring clay-mind like Gumby's deals in diversion, never gets deterred on the way. Gumby goes crazy over new prospects for play before figuring it all out. In over his head but no stopping him. In **Toy Joy,** he spots a monster of a hobbyhorse and climbs aboard even though he can't hold on to the reins. Whoa! Some close-ups of the rockin' bronc show that he's very much into horsing around. After the ride, a dizzy Gumby is unable to walk a straight line.

How not to trap Gumby? Get his drift. Whether roaming around as an interna-

In a Fix. *Gumby has access to all the heaviest equipment.*

Playtime

tional adventurer or as the playboy on the toy shop shelf, its only a movement—moving on. That's the Gumby difference.

Let's say right away who it is that just won't play. The green guy meets these types on his journeys to **The Small Planets.** The kid who won't share his train, holding the line so that no one else can get on board. The girl who frightens people away, monstrously. Or the nerd who doesn't know how to have a good time—too keyed up about his piano arpeggios.

The Gumby key, of course, is to never stop playing. Whether it's taking to the field for a backwards ninth inning of sandlot baseball with **The Gumby League** or kicking up some dirt for a **Racing Game.**

Contests that make things a toss-up leave the outcomes to chance landings. Stop on a black square—POP!—you disappear. Land on a green "X" and good luck—go to the head of the heap. Hit a red circle—pass the time while everyone passes.

But Gumby pastimes are just getting started. Start with the basics. The green guy has an inexhaustible inquisitiveness and more than a few piles of playthings—Erector Sets, Tinker Toys, Lincoln Logs, building blocks of all colors and sizes. And Gumby has access to all the heaviest equipment: cranes, cement mixers, tractors, plows, conveyor belts. Putting them all together, Gumby is puttering around in the shop. Never standing still, but with time on his hands to tinker with toys, goof around.

In **Toying Around,** Gumby stands by while a truck crashes into a huge tower of tiny bricks. Gumby fun is putting the pieces

Gumby Racer. *The chase is on, running on after.*

back up again. **In a Fix,** Gumby corrals his pony pal with a line of Lincoln Logs, only to blast it all apart again with a back-firing cannon. And during their North Pole visit, Gumby and Pokey crash into an igloo. Finishing the reconstruction—putting the icing on the cake—they watch as the mail plane again breaks the ice.

Building and breaking and building and breaking. The cycle never stops in this labor of love. Nothing to be done with, but everything to be done over. It's all a part and all a piece of a game that simply cannot cease.

The name of the game: tossing stuff up in the air and seeing where it all falls. Letting loose structures. Fabricating toy joy from what's at hand. Utilizing the use-less. Gumby welcomes everyone to join in the fun. Toys are prime, primo, all the time. And all the world—it's a game. Played out.

The Racer's Edge

The chase is on, running on after. What follows—a crash course through some chase escapades. Tracing the mechanics of the chase scene: an overdose of speed, an overkill of physical comedy. Spills and thrills. Motor mania and mayhem. These are racing games that raise the risks. Knockabout adventure.

Speed—a key to the racer's frame of mind. His dynamics. **Motor Mania** sets a frantic, frenetic pace for its kinetics. Stuck-up rich kid Reggie Van Snoot, with a "high-powered racing car" to boot, gets off to a fast start. Then when Gumby and Pokey's go-carts run out of go-go-go, he moves out to an even bigger lead. But the clayboys employ teamwork to get themselves back in the race. Pokey parks himself on the car frame with Gumby riding on top. By the finish line they're in

Lion Drive. *All in all, some pretty off-the-wall driving.*

front. Extra horsepower gives them the racer's edge.

But too much speed spells out of control. A carful of uncareful chases. **Lion Drive** takes a joyride with unlicensed Richard the Lion. Spotting a sporty auto, Richard scents adventure. "Oh boy! That's just the thing to see the world in." Thrill-seeking Gumby and Pokey agree to hop in. Only problem is that Richard's driving them all backward. A rocky ride in reverse, followed by a quick shift to fast forward with no pause for breath. Richard hits hairpin turns, careens around buildings. All in all, some pretty off-the-wall driving. A cut to a bird's-eye view of Gumbopolis reveals a-maze-ing patterns in motion. A smash through walls, up through floors, and out the door. Fall out. Poor Richard is left holding the wheel, and Pokey is flat tired in a crash landing.

Like **Lion Drive,** all great chase scenes must end with a bang. These movements of much-too-much motion flirt with disaster. Gumby's dog Nopey is on a motorized skateboard but doesn't seem to have a handle on it. **Dog Catchers** Gumby and Pokey try to nab Nopey as he whizzes on by, but fall flat on their faces. When they take to their cars for the all-out puppy hunt, they crash fast.

They call it slapstick and these chases make for smiling faces. Take the falls in the house of the **Haunted Hot Dog.** Complete with madcap silent music, a white-sheeted ghost of a Nopey shadows Gumby and Pokey. The scaredy-cats are chasing their tales when a knockdown fight uncovers the comic blunders.

Chases: follow-ups and afters. Nonstop action with no idling. The chase scene is the vehicle for so many zany adventures. Brake-ups to keep laughing. Spin-outs that take Gumby along for the ride. After the crack-up in **Dog Catchers,** Nopey shuts off the skateboard motor. Prickle: "He thought we were playing." Gumby: "Having fun." Like all adventure. The chase is on—catch it.

Tricky Trains

Gumby knows lots of ways to get up and go. Fire engines, ambulances, jeeps, trucks, and even planes take Gumby away from it all. But Gumby's preferred mode of transportation is riding the rails. Hitching like a hobo on any train that toots by. Traveling backward or forward—in any direction the engine takes him.

When Trixie the tricerotops's **Egg Trouble** brings her to the toy shop shelf, Gumby proudly points out his favorite toy. "That's a train!" he cries. Given half a chance, the gumboy will always choose a choo-choo.

In **Toy Joy** and **Toy Crazy,** Dad lets Gumby pick whatever he wants for a special birthday bonus. The green guy doesn't take stock of the options for too long. He and Pokey slam on the brakes as their convertible hits a crossing where a tiny freight engine has stopped, steaming like mad. Gumby jumps out and looks down the line. Pokey stokes the clayboy's fire: "Nah, that's too small for you." Just what Gumby needs to hear. He shrinks dinky and climbs aboard the iron horse.

After riding around, Gumby piles the train and its tracks into the back of his ambulance for safekeeping. That's exactly the object of his affections, the plaything he wants to possess to celebrate his clayday. But you can't get trains off the track just like that. When Gumby turns his back, the tooter knocks open the back doors and comes out smoking. Trains are pretty tricky that way, and even harder to track down. Them's the breaks.

Some engines come in boxes. In crates and cartons from the Gumbopolis Gadget

Works and from the Flakey Flakes cereal company. But out of the box you'll never see the end of it, if ever again.

Gumby has firsthand experience with this sort of **Train Trouble.** His brandnew steam engine rams forward and batters through the box. Catching it with a crane, Gumby sets the steamer between a pair of blocks—but they topple. "Slow" signs just get up and go. Gumby finally cows it with matador cape and hat, but even that won't catch the cowcatcher.

He's tried it all when it comes to corralling train cars. Gumby puts his foot down in **Foxy Box** and later takes to plain holding back the railroad car. No go—it just keeps going. No arresting by its rear. Wettest way to trap a train? Plop a watermelon on the tracks. No surprise. Even that idea is the pits.

Gumbasian trains keep a-rolling without switches, signals, or schedules. Taking up their tracks behind them and dropping new rails as they sail on by. Going around in circles. Roaring in reverse and off into the horizon.

As **Train Trouble** ends, Gumby sits back and decides to yield. He pats the floor, motioning for the engine to stop beside him, if only for a moment. Gumby pets the train, hitches up on its back, and gets in the cab. Gumby and his train: a couple—uncoupled. Gumby in training—no restraining.

Shooting for the Stars

Gumby's moon loony. A starry-eyed green guy who can't help but dream about orbs where no man has gone before. It's the ultimate enterprise—with the unknowing Gumby setting his sights on the great unknown. All kinds of planet plans. Shooting himself into outer space for a fantastic voyage.

Gumby on the Moon, sitting and star-

Train Trouble. *Gumby and his train: a couple—uncoupled.*

The Small Planets. *A starry-eyed green guy who can't help but dream about orbs where no man has gone before.*

ing. Mooning over all this . . . space. Rising from his rock, the rock starts to rock and rove. It's alive. A whole pile of these startling pyramid creatures, bug-eyed and armed, are after him. Sneaking up closer every time he turns his back, emerging from the moon shadows. The bug-eyes almost outrun him when Gumby remembers the sky's no limit. IIe tosses his gravity weights ahead and makes one giant leap over their heads.

Still roaming on the moon—**Trapped on the Moon**—Gumby's once again cornered by these pyramids. But cutting an adventure short never suits a clayboy's space, so Gumby again takes off what's holding him down, using his weights to bowl the bug-eyes aside. Rolling over and over through moon rivers and ravines, he lands deep in a lunar crater. It's dark and cold. Lights! Camera! Action! Starsearcher Dad peers through his telescope lens and spots this battle beyond the stars. "Yup, he's on the moon all right." Dad zips up and rides a fire truck ladder to the sky, battling an angry asteroid along the way. Help on the way.

Gumby, meanwhile, watches as the bug-eyes shuttle down the crater walls. The super-star sci-guy sights his flipped-out father. "Hey, Dad! I'm down here. How did you get up there?" Dad doesn't notice the bug-eyes—they've stopped moving. But you gotta keep moving when you're

star trekking. "They're only pretending to be stone!" cries Gumby, and Dad's quick-freezing spray saves the day.

Wishing upon a star, anew. Pokey and Prickle come running to Gumby with their tales of **Moon Madness.** "Something's chasing me!" yells Pokey. He's seen a pair of feet attached to shapely stems doing the moonwalk. But Gumby has a saying for this story: "When there's a full moon, people start seeing things." Just what the green guy was looking for: more lunatics. Goo's got it straight: "Stranger and stranger."

Gumby—stranger in a strange land. Taking great steps for claykind. Building a moon car to get past the last frontier. "Why couldn't he just climb the hill?" asks Prickle. Pokey's reply: "Because he has rocks in his head." The moon rocks. Outta sight.

Home Ranger

When Gumby returns from the wilds, he's a somebody. The Gumby abode—an A-frame dream with two-car garage, plenty of yard space, and nice Mrs. Wheedle next door. "I'm home!" he cries, skating in the door. Mom will be in the kitchen washing the dishes and Dad's (of course) at work. Domestic life. A model family.

Hanging around at home makes for an awfully straight clayboy. Mom and Dad show him that he should never put off his chores around the house. A wise old owl wants to wise Gumby up with a fable about asking permission before doing something that may affect others. And Pokey fills Gumby with the knowledge that he mustn't overeat and that he should never steal food.

But **Grub Grabber Gumby** perhaps oversteps the limits of good taste. The sadistic Mr. Stuff—a scary bogeyman with Pokey's main features—forces a truckload of burgers, a tank car of pop, and a nonstop conveyor belt of ice cream cones down Gumby's throat. "Well, well, you look almost full," says Stuff as a silent Gumby slides down in the chair, ready to burst. Gumby breaks the record for getting the message.

And leave it to some **Eager Beavers** to build a dam that reeks wreckage. It overflows and the whole forest goes under. Gumby observes, "This is the craziest river I've ever seen." But the moral holds no water either. True, chopping down trees and building dams cut into other niches of the forest, but it's crazy to think a beaver won't build. All the logs won't fit together. Dammed if you do and damned if you don't.

Gumby may be taught not to bend the rules. Not to bend back trees or tear off pieces of the house. But this teaching and preaching—this dead-serious setting and making—has to involve a kind of breaking. To stop a **Robot Rumpus,** Dad has to get his hands dirty, diving into the

Robot Rumpus. *This dead-serious setting and making has to involve a kind of breaking.*

Chicken Feed. *Settling down for supper has become a shambles.*

flower pit to dispatch the last mechanical digger. The automaton slings him to the top of the house. Dad returns, battered but ready for more action. He takes a wrench through the chest and loses a hunk. Dad and Gumby finally scoop the robot out of his hole, tearing its head off in the process. If you want to set a good standard, you've got to make your mark.

Chicken Feed raises the roof on all this homely stuff. It starts out all in the family with the best of etiquette. Mom announces, "Dinner's ready!" Sitting down at the table to eat and exchange conversation, practical Dad encourages his son to raise his chicken Tillie for economic returns: "You have a good business sense, son." But son is too good a breeder—a super-feeder super-breeder. The house starts rocking. Having eaten Gumby's nuclear food, Tillie hits the ceiling, growing to monstrous proportions and laying super-sized eggs that smash Dad's brand-new car. Mom calls on law and order, ordering up the police and an animal doctor.

But Gumby forgets about good breeding in this call to adventure. He pets the sick chick, even takes it for a ride. Parents protect. Dad: "Stay away from it!" Mom: "Save my son!" Gumby just waves from above. Settling down for supper has become a shambles. Wrecking the homelife and its stability, Tillie's upbringing brings out a flexible design for clay living. Come back around to adventure, unbound for adventure.

Gumby Alchemist

Going for Gold

Gumby states his goal like the alchemists of old: "This is the road to the gold country." A yellow brick road—paving the way for the precious. You'll be struck by all the golden opportunities for adventure. Panning about, note that Prickle has the Midas Touch, winning a golden iguana in the National Pet Contest. Dig in further downstream and unearth **Gold Rush Gumby** going for and getting it.

Golden nuggets scattered about, but how did they get there? As every alchemist knows, metals fire up in the process. It's metal's turn. The spinning of cogs and wheels, of metal mechanisms constantly in motion. In **Lost and Found,** a gold coin—a fifty-cent piece—rolls and spins. Gumby pursues the loose money through a number of strange lands where metal bends out of shape.

Gold Rush Gumby. *This is the road to the gold country.*

When Gumby hits gold, it bends too. Gold enters into circulation—into common, everyday use. Pesky Indian Chief Running Bear has a toothache. **Gold Rush Gumby** steps in for the medicine man and pulls it off, pulls it out. Finding a place for the gold in a practical space—a gold filling. A very flashy move and everyone's smiling. In another exchange, gold transfigures everything into works of art. Just one touch and the golden Amulet of Dila transforms Gumby into a psychedelic sculpture. It's **Mystic Magic.**

Once gold starts turning it's hard to stop. In **Golden Gosling,** a goose lays golden eggs, starting a gold chain reaction. Locked up in prison, the goose is in the clutches of a witch's spell that arrests its flight and forces it to produce solid gold. An escape, and alchemist Gumby shakes things up. One, he throws together blue and red for a lovely golden liquid. Two, the goose guzzles it down and the spell is broken. Three, the eggs break too: they hatch gold chicks and the prospects look good. Turns for the better.

More turns, inward. A conversion process. When the green one accepts these turns he becomes an alchemic adept, using transformation of the exterior world for purposes of the inner. In **Mirrorland,** Gumby finds the spirit when he meditates on metal coins and their changes. Gumby considers the thin wisdom of his mirror image: "If it fell in here, it'd be so thin you'd never find it." Never-ending changes of fortune.

All these phases of turning and all these turns of phrasing. In Gumby alchemy what matters is just that: the fact of transmutation. The flow of energy. The golden rule—everything is dear because everything can become gold. All things are drawn into the Great Work. The perfected image of alchemy: Gumby in a pile of sand staring at a coin in his outstretched hand. A happy return. Many happy returns.

Magic Touch

Gumby has the magic touch. The magic is his unfathomable power to make things (dis)appear. And the touch is divine—a laying on of hands. To heal. On the one hand, the magician; on the other, the shaman. Two roles that the little green guy handles with ease.

In **Magic Wand,** Gumby wields a wand—the instrument at hand for all magicians. Professor Hocus Pocus gives him some pointers: he pulls a penny and then a watch from nowhere, and hands Gumby a wand of his own to make any wish come true. Later, back at the lemonade stand, Mom's pitcher lies in pieces. A magic formula, a wave of the wand, and in the blink of an eye it's as good as gold. Pokey's pretty impressed. Gumby deals an off-hand remark: "Just a little magic trick I learned." The hand is quicker than the eye.

Potions and powders border the line between the magic man and the medicine man. Tricked up, mixing up, fixing up. Colonel Dixieman's Miracle Growth Stimulator in **A Lovely Bunch of Coconuts** and **The Zoops'** wizard's concoction can conjure watermelons out of coconuts and crazy crawling creatures out of watermelons. And Gumby's on hand through it all. Gumby's special gas turns his jalopy into an airplane to cruise over **The Hidden Valley.** As usual, he's along for the ride.

This shaman handiwork depends in large measure on staying in touch with the earth, on cultivating its secrets. He starts **Rain Spirits** in a swimming pool, diving right through the bottom and popping out of the ground to begin his adventure with Hopi the Indian. Gumby helps Hopi contact the spirit kachinas to seek rain for the crops. Hopi says, "You have to believe in the gods to see them," and Gumby feels the faith.

The rain responds, and the crops do too. Gumby is, after all, **The Fantastic Farmer**—with emphasis on the fantasy. When he's tilling the soil he's fielding out the territory of the marvelous. His turf. He can grow anything, any way, using his green thumb. And when he splits himself, he's doing the work of a hundred hired hands.

You've got to hand it to him, though Gumby may not have a clue. Holding on to the stuff of life, curing geese and dragons alike. He'll be just passing by, saying hi, and inanimate objects spring to life. He pulls off the oldest tricks in the book. Nothing in hand, Gumby reaches behind his back. Presto! It's an egg. Gumby delivers the goodies. A very charming green guy. Not slight, these sleights of hand.

Tripping Out

Gumby alchemy deals with psychedelia. Not only is the alchemist a trickster, he's a tripster too. Gumby drugs are mind-altering, expanding. **The Golden Iguana,** hooked on Mexican herbs, and Tillie the chicken, high on super-feed, manifest gigantic growth.

But Gumby alchemical adventures never enter through a main vein. They have a hallucinatory glow to them. A green haze perhaps. They thrive on the power of suggestion. Gumby's spaced-out stories open up imaginations to a new reality charged with metaphor and metamorphosis. A hinting tone is what's happening.

Some drugged-out scenes cast Gumby

The Magic Wand. *Hocus Pocus gives him some pointers.*

as a far-out farmer. His potent prescriptions have the potential to transform. A guru Gumby gives Pokey some roots to chew over. Pokey flips out, shoots through the color spectrum, and comes back red again. It's the drug trip in capsule form.

In **Of Clay and Critters,** Gumby sprinkles flower water on a bud and it starts sprouting, disseminating seeds that pop magically into little round critters who spout gibberish. When **Fantastic Farmer** Gumby throws some secret formula on the soil, the plants pop up in weird ways— very high in a hurry. Pokey reports, "Our crops grow up in a funny way now." Real dopey.

One final farming flashback. In **Gopher Trouble,** Gumby goes for it all. When the addicted gophers start injecting the corn with chemicals to sprout giant roots— supporting an ever-growing habit—Gumby develops an antidote. It's a kind of metha-

done treatment concocted in his lab to give the gophers a tasty substitute. This way, everybody can get his fix, get off/on his drug.

When these strange transformations start working, brains get fried, crispy. You can freak, give in to the fear of the unknown, even burn out. Once he's **In the Dough,** Gumby overhears the pastries plotting to make him into a pie filling. Other paranoid fantasies turn up. An old dough-head, pretty toasted, asks dealer Mr. Dough about the new kid in the oven. "Oh, that's Gumby. He wants me to show him how to bake." A chorus of dough boys break into hysterics. Peer pressure in the pressure cooker or a sudden burst of laughing gas? Gumby and his friends cook up golden brown—well done—with Mr. Dough a role model. Pokey's paralyzed? Flattened by a pie roller and lost on a cookie tray? Relax. "Oh don't worry,

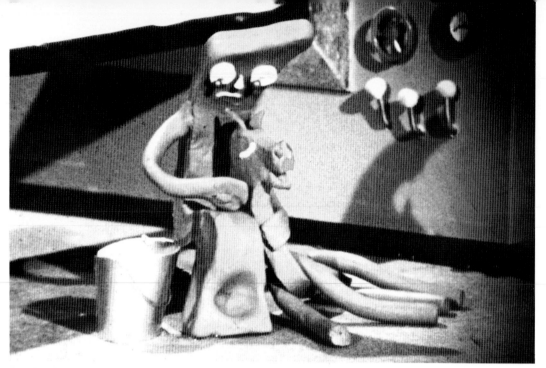

In the Dough. *He wants me to show him how to bake.*

he'll turn up somewhere," goes Dough. Gumby later tells Pokey in awe, "That's the same fellow who led us here, but he's been raised."

The green guy accepts the invitation to do dough, get pie-eyed. "He'll never be the same again," says Mom as the folks open the oven door. Gumby pops out of the jelly roll, fresh for just another high.

Machines

Clank. Crank. Gumby machinates, modulates, dreams up new mechanisms. Finetooling them, fooling around with them. Names from a fractured future: a Sub-Atomic Teleporter, a Sonic Vibratron, a Dust Generator and Disseminator.

Gumby mumbo jumbo—high-tech lingo for some very strange toys. "Something that will revolutionize the transportation industry," that "analyzes atomic structure" with "micro-analytical cells." Gobbledygook that "explains" these motors, these nonsense machines. These rockets that run on "fuel, LOX [liquid oxygen], and bagels." These teleporting rigs where you

can walk from station to station in the time it takes to beam across. Einstein's rolling in his grave as the green guy underplays: "I haven't figured that out yet."

Figure that. He built it but doesn't know how it works. He slapped this and that together, push-pulled the buttons and levers, but can't begin to control the result. Something escapes Gumby—some logic. Conducting studies in viscosity in **Missile Bird** to create the world's toughest net, Gumby gets bested by this flighty flying object. The mesh may not quit, but neither will the rocket. Gumby meets a brick wall at breakneck speed. A scientific breakthrough.

Machines keep moving. A motion, perpetual. Mystifying modes of operation. Endlessly huffing and puffing, beeping and bonking. Shooting out flags, flashing lights for no apparent reason, taking up space to simply get turned on.

Just punch it up on the software and the **Do It Yourself Gumby** watchama-callit's got the program. An infinite data base processes and produces a turkey, piano, tiger, cage, and mini-robot in quick

Yard Work Made Easy. *A retrofitting that never finds a stop.*

succession. Until robot grabs hold of the knobs and turns out thingamabobs at an ever more manic pace. Beyond any consumer's dreams.

Springs twist round and round and pop loose, gears start turning backward. The robots start a rumpus in Gumby's backyard. The automatons paint windows instead of walls, trash the garage rather than pick up trash, rip out plants, leaving the weeds. Pretty wild.

At the outer limits lies perhaps the screwiest machine. Pokey pops the question: "What's that fancy contraption?" Gumby's the proud parent. "It's a Sub-Atomic Teleporter." A sci-fi like device moving matter from one space to another with nothing in between. Disconnecting, reconnecting, combining faster than the speed of light. Pop Pokey into one chamber and he's blossomed a flowerpot tail out the other. Or Pokey goes bald trading mane for tail. It's a tale of realignment. Pokey and Gumby swap tops and bottoms in all possible permutations. A Gumboma-

taur? Half horse, half green guy. Whatever the fit—always on, all systems go. A retrofitting that never finds a stop. Micro or macro, Gumby's in transports.

Kingdom of Roo

Time and again Gumby finds himself in the Middle Ages—in a world of kings, knights, damsels in distress, and, of course, wizards. He spells out his status in the kingdom in **Rain for Roo** when he proclaims, "I am a scientist, not a wizard. I know something about rain. The wizard just guesses." A green Connecticut Yankee, wearing a mortarboard, hurled into Roo with a toy shop arsenal to do battle.

Sometimes Gumby turns tidbits of nature knowledge to his advantage. Coaxing the heavens to rain because he knows how to seed the clouds. When the rain turns to red mud, Gumby need only run a quick analysis before shouting "Eureka!" His profound discovery? It's raining metal.

Iron. "You can make all kinds of things with iron: nails, hammers, plows, pots, kettles, wheels, knives, forks, spoons, and thousands of other things!"

Gumby science is simple: beat the bad guys of old with the world of the new. But in Roo the new looks mighty peculiar. Foregoing a lance, Gumby zaps the Black Knight in **King for a Day** using a water pistol filled with grape juice. **Mysterious Fires**? No problem. Gumby rides his fire truck to the kingdom and cools off the hot-headed dragon. **The Black Knight** back to steal the throne? The green guy drives an Erector Set crane and super-magnet to the jousting field, stripping Blackie down to his drawers.

But here, there, and everywhere, Gumby refuses to fight on sensible terms. He keeps divesting himself of horse and armor because, like logic, it's much too confining. Gumby prefers to set a wayward, mind-boggling course. Take **Sad King Ott's Daughter,** when Gumby and Pokey bring the magic morph—a changeling— to the kingdom. The clayboy's crazy plan to save Ott's daughter involves changing the morph from a marble into a wedding cup, and later, once it's inside Blackie's castle, into an elephant!

What sort of science is this? One that never lets Gumby down. Never brings him back to earth. For all this science talk's a pure puff of smoke. Prickle calls him "The world's best spell-breaker." The White Knight: "Sir Magician, Green Sir." King Ott: "The Knight of the Fire Engine." It appears that everyone already knows. When it comes to Gumby science, the effect is sheer wizardry.

Thinking Kap

When Gumby's stumped he puts on his thinking cap and studies with a scholar pal. Responding to trouble, Gumby resolves: "I'll call up my friend Professor Kap. He seems to know everything." *Seems* to know? Something seems awry here. Is Kap a know-it-all or is he a mere dissembler? For Kap, knowledge becomes a big question mark.

Who is this chap named Kap? A big head on a bulbous body. He comes across not as a mad scientist so much as your jovial but bumbling inventor-uncle, full of half-baked ideas still in the fire. A cuddly, funny figure. Pondering matters, forever studying things from all sides. In his lab you'll find him scratching his head, a bit absentminded, his fluffy white hair a-puffing. Kap's another pseudo-scientist, the ace alchemist.

But does Kap lapse? After all, we encounter him in many situations that backfire. Investigating some chemical gunk in **G.F.D. (Gumby Fire Department)** that blows up in his face and sets his lab ablaze. Or his hair-raising formula, another comic Kap-tastrophe. He manages to give Gumby a hipster look, but Prickle gets a pain in his honker when a horn grows instead of a cookie duster.

The list goes on . . . Kap feeds **The Golden Iguana** a special batch of his Mexcian herbs and iguana goes Godzilla on the gang. He devises a super-spray to shrink troubles down to size but ends up as an Incredible Expanded Man.

But seeing messed-up missions misses the captial point. There are no solutions in his chemicals. Kap's vision: life without ends, ongoing. Kap's supposed "errors" are testimonies to transformation, the surprises life sets in store, sets us up for. "He'll have a wonderful time trying to figure out how to make the iguana smaller," Gumby remarks.

Sans solutions, these backfires inspire. Explosions with no negative feedback. Kap captivated by everything. To recap. Kap's

Mysterious Fires. *Beat the bad guys of old with the world of the new.*

last rap: "Who knows what new inventions I can think up? This bigger head means a bigger brain too." Who knows?

Test Time

Without poisons and antidotes, Gumby and his friends find a substitute, a fresh way to skate through life. Gumby adventures opt for testing. Whatever the reactions, Gumby never stops experimenting. In this lab there are test tubes filled with chemical mixtures made for mix up. Playing at science and theosophy, he's sending up trial (and error) balloons, throwing out magic feelers. In the dark, for fun, not for profit.

As **The Fantastic Farmer,** Gumby agrees to help Farmer Glenn straighten

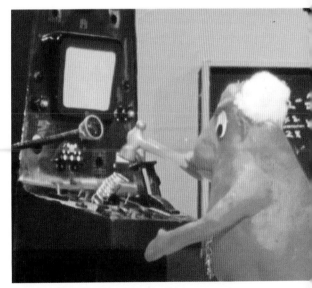

Space Ball *(a Professor Kap special).* *Explosions with no negative feedback.*

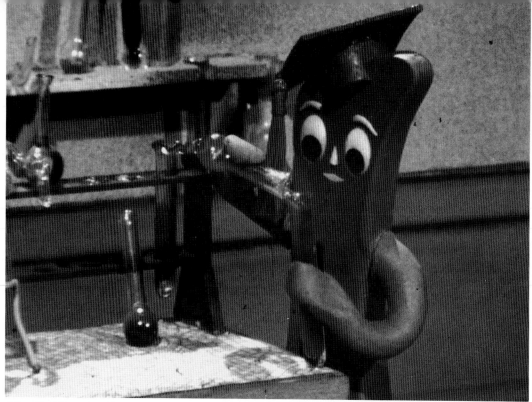

The Golden Gosling. *Test tubes filled with chemical mixtures made for mix up.*

out his crops. Gumby hits the lab—a gigantic chemistry set—and ventures a guess. How about a bit of this and some of that? Blam! The clayboy explodes black. In the background the words "Fun with Chemistry" loom large. Time to check out a few textbooks for some on-the-job research. Another attempt with a blue vial, but still no help for the corn. Oh well, back to the drawing board.

Gumby goes for trouble in **Gopher Trouble** and undertakes an extraordinary project—synthesizing food using a handle and a wooden box with two holes. He pounds on it with a hammer and throws some straw in to make it go. Gumby feeds the result to Pokey, who nearly expires. Hmm. Needs more investigating. He hammers and drills in a new round of modifications.

Gumby drills holes in time as well as timber. Tests elude tense, suspend the need to get things done. He's got until five to come up with some new root-

manufacturing process for the gophers. A race against time, with a troublemaking cuckoo counting down the minutes to go. Gumby finally reaches over and nails the cuckoo door shut. No more time.

It's the time for adventure—on the move out of the present. **Tail Tale**'s Sub-Atomic Teleporter adds new dimensions to space-time at three times the speed of light. It's also a time for absolute relativity. The menacing **Big Eye** in the germ's sky turns out to be Gumby looking through a microscope, even though he's also down with the germs. As above, so below: what's looked at is also looking in.

Alchemy taking shape. Transmuting objects—mutating time. A time warp. These experiments with unsettling solvents, these impossible dreams that Gumby creates for himself. Gumby alchemy—a hypothetical somewhere far off and over. Where the test counts much more than the rest. A speculative science with its head in the clouds. Gumby's good time.

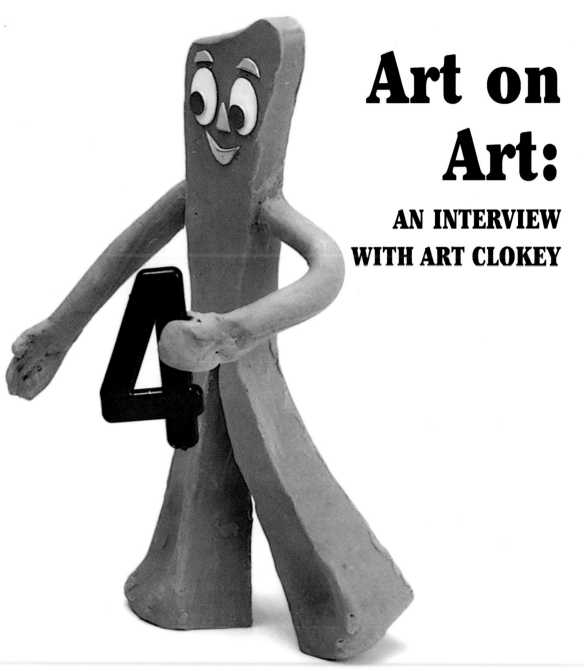

Art on Art:

AN INTERVIEW WITH ART CLOKEY

What's in a name? Names like Gumby, Gumbasia, and Gumbopolis? Or Art Clokey? We chatted with Art and his wife, Gloria, on their back porch about all these names and the bits and pieces of words within them. Single syllables, puns, rhymes. A question each about *are, cloak, clock, lock, key, look, low, low key, gum, um, bas, Asia, ba, gumbo, a, op, pol, polis, po, is, be.* And other questions on Art.

LOUIS: The first word is *are*. How are you?

ART: (holding on to his pony pal Pokey): I'm fine. Though my voice is a little hoarse.

LOUIS: See if you can voice an opinion on this word—*cloak*. Cloaks are worn, they also get worn out. Gumby is going on thirty years old and he's very fashionable. How do you explain the fact that the films still look so brand-new after thirty years?

ART: Well, technically they were shot on good color film that didn't fade with age.

LOUIS: Do you think that color is the key reason why they look so fresh?

ART: No, no. It's clay—which is very basic in the psyche as a substance. Scientists say that we evolved from clay. It's been in our civilization for years as a medium for expression and a very practical medium—making pots for carrying water, storing grain, and used as writing tablets for many thousands of years.

What else? Birds use clay to build their nests. Oh, little images and gods, of course. And Jesus used clay to heal.

LOUIS: Images and gods like Gumby. Have you ever thought what other images in other cultures are likened unto Gumby? Or that Gumby is likened unto?

ART: Well, the Hopi Indians have a tradition about a green man (laughs).

SCOTT: And there's also the leprechaun in the Irish tradition.

LOUIS: And the Mexican Mescalito.

SCOTT: Maybe there's something that you're feeding into . . .

LOUIS: Like an archetype.

ART: Yeah. If they were stories that were told to every generation, that's possible.

LOUIS: So you've reached some kind of mythic pulse.

ART: Some people think so (laughs).

SCOTT: And Gumby also has the capacity to enter stories—to stage myths of his own making.

ART: I can remember a book I had as a child. The first page showed somebody

Rain Spirits. *Maybe there's something Gumby feeds into . . . like an archetype.*

shooting a gun. When you turned the page, you saw the bullet go through a clock in a house. Turn another page and it went through somebody's hat, and so on. The idea of this bullet going through the whole neighborhood and the hole running from the first page of the book to the last fascinated me. I guess that's where I got the idea of Gumby walking into books.

SCOTT: The next word is *clock*. It's a clock instead of a cloak.

ART: Do you know where that's derived from? "Clokey" is derived from "clocher." It's "to ring a bell" in French. It got changed to "Cloque" in England and it changed to "Clokey" in Scotland. There was a ballad over there called "The Clokeys and the Campbells."

SCOTT: Is there a way that you've ever thought of yourself as ringing the bell?

ART: My foster father played the organ and was a musician. Part of the organ is the chimes, of course. Ringing bells has a lot of symbolism for me.

SCOTT: In what way?

ART: Ringing bells of awareness in a person's heart. It strikes something—a chord.

SCOTT: Well, my clock question has to do with time, and Gumby's adventures depend on good timing. How is it that you let the good times roll?

ART: It's similar to music. You build to a climax through use of timing and intensity of the stimuli—the duration, syncopation, and so on. All deal with the same thing. Slavko Vorkapich, my film teacher at USC, taught that it's more like poetry and music. He would refer to the shots and the definite cuts as notes. Visual notes to combine and use in various ways, to get across your feelings. To delight and create new ideas and things—a new slant on life. You can do amazing things to the autonomic

Gumby Crosses the Delaware. *We think that he's revealed it, but the soldiers take it as a joke.*

nervous system if you know how to organize these forces. It's the balancing of repetition, variety, tempo. And just a split second of rest. It's all a mysterious combination.

LOUIS: Are mystical notions about balancing attachment and detachment in life a kind of parallel there?

ART: Right, you're picking up on it. I've read Sai Baba mention something like that. Cloak—there's a certain artistic factor of cloaking.

SCOTT: Tell us about it.

ART: You cloak something until you want to reveal it and then people are surprised.

LOUIS: Would you say that art is a kind of game that involves disclosures and concealments? Holding out the carrot?

ART: Sure. And sometimes we let you in on it, like in **Gumby Crosses the Delaware.** The Hessians don't know that George Washington is coming across the Delaware at night, but we do. And we identify with Pokey, who's trying to keep it a secret from the Hessians. We think that he's revealed it, but the sol-

Gumby chess set. Life is a game: play it.

diers take it as a joke. They keep fooling themselves and we are in on it.

SCOTT: Is it just a constant game?

ART: Yeah. Life is a game: play it. That's what Sai Baba keeps telling people. But the cloaking, the surprise factor, is interesting. I remember my own children. The first thing they really loved was surprise. Peek-a-boo, hide and seek, stuff like that. That's suspense: is it going to turn out this way or that way? How is it going to happen? What's going to happen next? That's the surprise. In the simplest of clowning actions, when Gumby falls into a toaster, when you hear it go click, click, click . . . you don't know what he's going to look like when he pops out.

LOUIS: Being kept in suspense and being surprised. That's related to what it means to be a child—experiencing the world that way.

ART: Yeah, the joy. The key to life and joy is surprise. The game is to keep a certain part of your life a secret.

LOUIS: Now we'd like to talk about language, and the word is *lock*. Words get locked together, and that is a play of language. What are four or five of your favorite puns?

ART: Well, there you have me at a disadvantage because I'm very bad at remembering jokes and puns.

SCOTT: But you tell puns all the time. You're always punning.

ART: But that comes from the subconscious, not from the memory. I guess that's the point of it.

LOUIS: That the pun can only work situation by situation.

ART: Pun is fun.

SCOTT: That's good. Louis has a favorite . . .

LOUIS: I always say tea is key.

SCOTT: And that may have to do with the next word, which is *key*. We know you've been a student of spiritual teachers like Sathya Sai Baba, Walt Whitman, Alan Watts, and Muktananda.

ART: "Mukti" is liberation.

SCOTT: Well, the question is—and this is the biggest question we can ask you, Art—tell us, what is the key to the mysteries?

ART: The key is in the lock (much laughter). I don't feel like turning it at this moment.

SCOTT: Have you ever told that one before?

ART: No, it's just an accident. Life is an accident.

LOUIS: The next word is *look,* which is very important to a film maker—looking, seeing, viewing. You say that your first choice for a career would have been to be a big Hollywood film maker shooting Sophia Loren and all the starlets. Now picture and describe for us a good-looking woman, and does it help to have a camera?

ART: Well, a camera would get in the way (chuckles). Naturally, there's a sensuous nature to certain types of filming. Maybe I'll have to show you the almost pornographic film I once made. Because of my upbringing I had a certain timid-

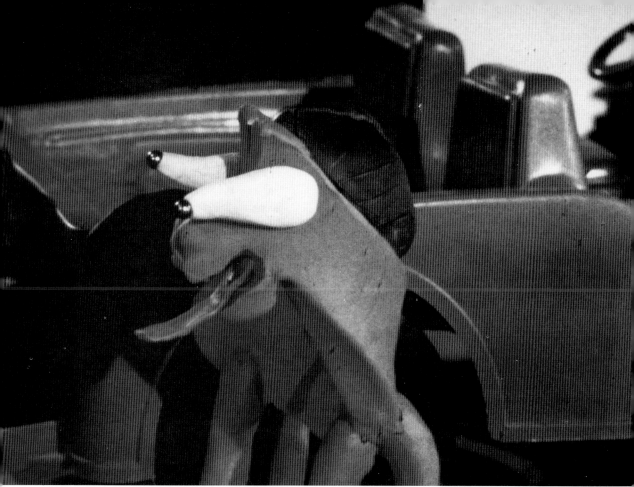

The Glob. _You're going to make everyone a voyeur._

ity—a certain lack of self-confidence—that inhibited my self-assertion. So I felt that the camera was a way that I could assert myself without getting out in front of people and being vulnerable.

LOUIS: Again the operation of disclosing yourself and concealing yourself. You can control, assert, and shoot, yet you are hidden behind the lens.

SCOTT: Many people have noted that the whole experience of watching a movie is voyeuristic. Sitting in the dark room . . .

ART: You're going to make everyone a voyeur.

SCOTT: Well, aren't we all?

ART: No, I think the voyeur is the person who watches another person enjoy himself because he's afraid to get in there and enjoy himself and get hurt.

SCOTT: And yet you remain a movie maker,

the person who wants to make these kinds of fantasies for others.

ART: We say it's a form of art.

SCOTT: It's kind of complicated, isn't it?

ART: It's part of the mystery of positive and negative, of good and bad, of limited and unlimited. It's interesting.

SCOTT: You grew up not only steeped in gumbo but also in slapsticky, _low_ kinds of comedy. What's so funny?

ART: "What is funny?" Well, we're going into an analysis of comedy here. I remember I was really fascinated with the Soupy Sales show. He used this gimmick—a filmic device—that I had learned under Vorkapich. He'd open a door and instead of going into another room he'd cut in such a way that he'd go into an airplane or step out onto a cliff.

LOUIS: Like that Keaton film where the background keeps changing and he doesn't know where he is.

ART: A juxtaposition of completely different locales and yet joining them by movement.

LOUIS: And that is a basic principle of montage. Why is the viewer going to laugh when he sees that scene?

ART: Surprise is part of it. What's so funny . . . I remember Alan Watts discussed this and said humor is something like turning two video cameras on each other; lock them eye to eye and you get nothing but the titillation of the snow or whatever it is. There's nothing there. It's the center of the onion. So life is just one big laugh underneath. If you're really hip.

LOUIS: So slapstick is about falling into piles of mud and laughing (laughter). Our next phrase is *low key*. Is Art Clokey a low-key kind of guy?

ART: Maybe that should be asked of my wife and partner.

GLORIA: Yes, he is. The thing that amazes me about Arthur is that he's done this wonderful thing creating Gumby and he doesn't really think it's that big. He's just very low key about it. He says, "Some people are house painters, some people are plumbers, and I made Gumby. And so what? I did something I happened to fall into" (laughs).

ART: I'm not clear in my mind what is low key.

LOUIS: Low key has something to do with the distinction between prickly and gooey. Gooey is easygoing, low key . . .

ART: Well maybe I'm "pruey" (much laughter).

SCOTT: *Gum.* Everyone talks to you about gumbo and sticky mud. We're going to ask you about something just a bit different. Louis, for example, likes the clean taste of Dentyne cinnamon gum,

Gumby Business. *It's been so long since I chewed gum.*

and we're wondering if you have a favorite gum and why?

ART: (laughing) It's been so long since I chewed gum.

SCOTT: Next you're going to tell us you don't like ice cream cones.

ART: That's more like it. I love hot fudge sundaes with real whipped cream and nuts. That's the best substitute for sex I've ever found.

SCOTT: Do you ever have to watch yourself in terms of getting too cold and losing your flexibility after you've eaten too many ice cream cones—say if you've eaten 100 ice cream cones at a time?

ART: I'm not like Gumby in that respect. I expand; he becomes rigid.

LOUIS: The next word is *um* (pause). A pause. The saying goes: "The pause that refreshes." A pause as in stop-action animation. Tell us about taking breaks between shots.

ART: I never take umbrage.

SCOTT: Then on we go. The next word is *bas,* as in bas-relief. One way to describe it is a sculpture in three dimensions but with only one way of seeing it, unlike a sculpture on a pedestal. We're wondering if the camera too involves a kind of definite and defined point of view, a single way of seeing. And if not, what's the camera about?

ART: It's just a single eye.

LOUIS: What kind of eye? A third eye?

ART: It's like looking at life through a keyhole. That's what Edward R. Murrow said about cinema. It's funny, but when I was taking carbogen—70 percent oxygen and 30 percent CO_2—the visions I had breathing that gas were a lot like movies in that they faded in and out. It was like a panoramic view.

SCOTT: The next word is *Asia,* and we know you've spent a lot of time traveling. Your first movies were made in Siberia and you've made trips to India and Japan. What is it about being an adventurer that you like?

ART: Constant variety; freedom from responsibilities, I guess. Not really being involved in anything. Just voyeurs . . . voyaging. Voyaging voyeurs.

SCOTT: That's the title for an episode!

LOUIS: Do you have any travel tips for the would-be Asian traveler or explorer?

ART: Well if you go to India and you'd like to see God, I'd suggest that you go to Puttaparthi, or Whitefield, which is just outside Bangalor. Isn't it outrageous to say that? But this Sai Baba claims to be God and he's substantiating his claim day after day.

LOUIS: Then let's look at *ba.* Baba. On the subject of the avatar, describe for us the connection between a Baba and a Gumba.

ART: That's interesting. I remember where Gumby has his hands behind his back in **Egg Trouble.** He brings them around

Egg Trouble. *He materializes things right in his hands in full view of people.*

in front of him and there's a big egg, a dinosaur egg in his hand. Sai Baba does the same thing. He materializes things right in his hands in full view of people. He pulls his sleeves up for the skeptics so they can't say he brought it out of his sleeve. You just stand there a few feet away from him and you see this thing appearing in his hand like a necklace or a solid gold image of Krishna. And he's been doing this for forty, fifty years. A magician would go broke in a few months giving these things away.

SCOTT: So how would you characterize this similarity that you're talking about? That both Sai Baba and Gumby have the ability . . .

ART: Gumby reminds the child of who he is and where he came from. Like *Alice in Wonderland* or the land of the fairy tales, where anything can happen. And he reminds them that that's really the

way life is . . . but we can't see it. Our eyes are clouded with what is called *maya* in India; what we call lack of awareness. So the kid is reminded that he can do anything.

SCOTT: So again, you feel that's the same as Sai Baba.

ART: Yes. When Sai Baba was in grammar school he was like Gumby. He was very playful. He would run races, play pranks—magical pranks. Baba was being reprimanded by a teacher for something innocent so he made the teacher stick to the chair. And he would materialize candy and pencils and things from an empty paper bag for his friends. It wasn't in there, but somehow it came out.

LOUIS: How about *gumbo*? We would like you to give us a good vegetarian recipe to get souped up.

ART: We found this wonderful vegetable

Art Clokey at work in the studio. It tends to disintegrate the notions of perception.

protein powder that is 87 percent protein with all the essential vitamins. My wife, Gloria, can do that better than I. She makes wonderful soups. She creates them.

GLORIA: The main noningredient is the flesh of living creatures.

SCOTT: Is this soup composed mainly of noningredients?

GLORIA: No, that's the only noningredient. Anything else can go into it. Gumbasia beans, potatoes, carrots, onions, peas, tofu, Pokey noodles. I just thought of a name—"Tofu Gumbo."

ART: Hey, that's a great name.

SCOTT: Super!

ART: Super soup.

SCOTT: A super letter: *a* in Gumbasia. *A* is a singular article, the first letter of the alphabet. It's a kind of identity because it points out an ego, a thing. We're wondering if montage technique in film making questions the notion of identity.

ART: It tends to disintegrate the notions of perception. Montage is combining . . . taking images and putting them together in a certain way to create.

LOUIS: So it's a process that breaks down barriers between objects. One object claims to be an identity and another the same. Montage makes that separation impossible.

ART: I'd say it's a juggling of unities. Underlying every film, each cut or frame is a jolt.

SCOTT: Is film a kind of language?

ART: Naturally. It's just a juxtaposition of images.

LOUIS: Is there a difference between the verbal and film languages?

ART: They are both signifying practices. They're also tools. Tools of consciousness to expand the consciousness and play around with it.

LOUIS: We'd like to keep talking about film, continuing with the word *op*. You make movies—flicks—optical illusions. Should they flicker?

ART: Isn't that funny? Many times we discussed the irony that there's no such thing as a motion picture. There's no motion. In television it's just a dot—the dot moves. You could stop the images of the televison just as you could stop the light in stop-action. We create the motion in our brains, so we are it.

LOUIS: Do you see the flickering of light in film making related somehow to the light of enlightenment?

ART: Yeah. I thought about that in relationship to what I've been learning from Sai Baba and the other gurus. It's all light. Some light is invisible. There are invisible forms of energy. We're viewing only very limited bands of light that our eyes pick up. Some people can pick up other bands. I'm amazed at some of the things they can see . . . auras and stuff like that. In movies, you create with light. You do a little dance for the eyes—like fireworks. Fireworks are all light, and you know how exciting explosions are. That was the feeling we were trying to convey on the screen. I looked upon making motion pictures as a kind of parable of existence, of consciousness.

SCOTT: Then any film maker is a basic sort of consciousness raiser because the film maker is always showing what it means to have vision.

LOUIS: Or you could say that the veil of maya is torn away by the film maker who is able to shoot through to light.

ART: Well, he's using light to give the illusion of substance, which is really inside us. You see, the projector is the atman or the brahman that is projecting all these ego things. It's a parable of god consciousness. It's the whole pro-

Art Clokey dressed for his and Gloria's 1974 TV series, Arthur and Guenevere. *I thought, O.K., God is Shakespeare, but we have all these characters.*

cess with the camera, the projector, the screen. I've thought about that many times. Film has the secret of existence more than any other art form. Movies carry a lesson: we create. The atman in us creates everything. Project out and see—see what we create (pause). I'm beginning to think that I've been on an LSD trip or something.

LOUIS: Being a film maker, a projector of images, is a parable then of how the mind creates the universe.

ART: It is the ultimate parable. Do we really exist as entities? That brahman is everything. And he or it or she is thinking all these thoughts. You're just a thought. I'm just a thought. Everything is just a wonderful new thought and the god is in us experiencing the diverse nature of pretending. It's like kids pretending. We tend to forget. Who

are you? I used to go with my father to the Pasadena Playhouse and see Shakespeare's plays. I thought, O.K., God is Shakespeare, but we have all these characters. Iago is Shakespeare, Lear is Shakespeare. And yet Lear is Lear and Iago is Iago.

LOUIS: It's the same thing in **Who's What?** How do you sort out that Henry makes Rodgy but Rodgy is still Rodgy. But then Henry was made by the artist . . .

SCOTT: But the artist made Rodgy too . . .

LOUIS: But then who made the artist? What's going on? There's all these levels with all these kinds of projections.

SCOTT: Projecting out, the next word is *pol.* Polo. We notice that you wear a lot of Gumby clothes—for example, Gumby polo shirts. We've even on occasion seen you wear a Gumby bump. We're wondering, what defines Gumby fashion?

ART: What defines Gumby fashion? Fashion is really anti-Gumby.

SCOTT: Except, of course, that you always have to fashion clay, don't you?

ART: Well, that's a different connotation. That is a different thing from "What is the fashion today? What is she wearing that we can copy?"

LOUIS: But the fact that it's the same word makes these things bind together and makes them hard to distinguish.

ART: Like "molding."

LOUIS: Right. Molding is a perfect example. Molding clay, but being of the same mold. Some undecidability in the word, just like fashion.

ART: Words are fun.

GLORIA: Moldy bread.

LOUIS: Right. Moldy bread means it's lasted too long, but at the same time . . .

SCOTT: The bread is changing.

LOUIS: The next word is the Greek root *polis.* And the variation in English is not only *government,* but *police.* So we

The Gumby League. *Molding clay, but being of the same mold.*

want to know about any incidents or brushes with the law over the years that you would care to or maybe you don't care to remember.

SCOTT: This is kind of your civil disobedience question.

ART: I have had fantasies of great civil disobedience. When I got tickets for parking too long at a parking meter, I had fantasies. I was very tempted to go around destroying hundreds of these meters up and down Wilshire Boulevard by putting steel glue in the slots at night, and then all these people come and see the meters out of order in the morning.

SCOTT AND LOUIS (simultaneously): That's good.

SCOTT: The next little word is *po*—like po-faced, poker-faced. Since you're a cut-up at film and a former stand-up comic, we felt obliged to ask you: can anybody keep a straight face?

ART: Po for Pokey . . . but can anybody keep a straight face? In the face of what? We can play around with it. Straight face. Straitlaced. Straight-faced is straitlaced. Yeah.

LOUIS: The last question is a kind of Zen koan . . .

SCOTT: Combining our last two words . . .

LOUIS: The last two words are the *is* from Gumbopolis and the *be* from Gumby. You once said "Gumby just is." But if he is always changing, how can that be?

ART (laughs): That's the irony of existence. We is and we ain't. Is we or is we ain't? The nature of our essence is change. And a grew, be. Groobee.

LOUIS: Groobee doobee do.

ART: That has a lot of significance, but we can't get into that now or I'll freeze to death.

GLORIA: You didn't take your Gumbometer with you.

5 Gumby Zen Master

At Piece

Gumby smiles—even when **In a Fix.** His cannon has backfired, blowing him up black in the process. He is besieged by two alien, avocadolike characters who cling to him. He's still smiling. A stillness in the center—enlightenment. No reason, just the happy-go-lucky grin of a Zen master.

Fixated folk tie themselves down, too attached. Falling into desire traps. But a clayboy has to stay cling-free. It's a balancing act. Gumby, in **Toy Capers,** walks the high wire above the monorail in motion. Mastering the tightrope, Gumby swings and sways with the greatest of ease. An ongoing juggling, jostling.

He may be moved around but Gumby can never be touched. Folding in an accordion and not freaking out. It's **Gumby**

Business and it looks like a big pain. But not for this master of the Book of Changes. He accords with it. Touching his feet to the keys, feeling them spring back up. In harmony. Letting the instrument bend him back and forth and crush him paper-thin. A rigorous spiritual exercise. At piece with the world.

Opportunities for attachment entanglements arise with every Gumby adventure. Calling for a clayboy who can let go of himself. No ego. In **The Fantastic Farmer** he fractures. Dozens of Gumbys on tractors plowing Farmer Glenn's fields. A demonstration of selflessness rolled into one, many. It's the same tactic in **Gumby Concerto.** Since Too and Loo are in tears,

Gumby Business. *In harmony.*

The Fantastic Farmer. *A demonstration of selflessness rolled into one, many.*

Gumby divides into a chorus for a song-and-dance number that splits their sides with laughter.

Dividing into others as well. In **Too Loo,** Gumby gives desiring subject Mr. Sour Note a little Zen lesson on the illusions of the ego. Sour wants to net the notes, to apprehend them. Gumby takes on their attributes, assumes their identities. When Sour snaps the trap, Gumby goes green again and shows him who's captured.

Gumby's Buddhist calm could be equated with a loss of interest—passivity. But the green Zen master baffles activity with super-quick reaction time. Instantaneous reflexes. It's an art that just takes a little practice.

The **Tricky Ball** goes through many volatile transformations—in color, size, shape, volume—and Gumby rolls with the changes. An adaptable adept. When the ball grows, Gumby sits on it and rides with it. As soon as it runs him over and flattens him out, he's a-round till Gumby again. When the ball starts pulsing in his hands, Gumby acts detached to provide some extra-strength equilibrium. Gumby's absorbed. He stares intently at the ball as it undergoes its shifts. The meditative gaze intent, the mind is happy.

Or Gumby watches and waits with faces that won't be fazed by anything. A deadpan Gumby looks on and wonders as the ball disappears, comes back again, goes liquid. Gumby goes with the flow. The ball returns to its original size as a smiling Gumby and Nopey skate away from the play.

Any which way, reactions slide over into actions. Roll over. Methods of acting when the ball starts rolling and things get tricky. Ways to cope within the perpetual cycles, the generations of desire. Watch not-do-it-yourself Gumby. He's just having a ball.

Pigeon in a Plum Tree. *The kid wants to give his true love "something special." Ott thinks especially cheap.*

Pun-demonium

Clayboys are very punny. Pun masters who refuse to take language too seriously, attach names to things. Gumby takes

words as polymorphous materials for toying around. Plays on words. Turns a phrase as easily as a train wheel.

The first meeting of Gumby and Pokey in **Little Lost Pony** spells out the nature of this wisecracking relationship with language. What's your name? Pokey. What a funny name! Ah ha ha ha ha ha! What's your name? Gumby. He he he he he he he he! For their names' sakes, the close personal friends are rolling in the aisles. Here it's the toy shop floor, with both boys doubled over with laughter.

It's the other side that language tries to hide. In **Chicken Feed,** Mom and Dad sense the first rumblings of this disloca-

Pigeon in a Plum Tree. *Original storybook sketches.*

tion. The ground moves, Mom cries, "What on earth was that?" Dad's one-liner shakes things up. "Probably an earthquake." The pun comes home to roost, exploding with meaning. A bursting at the seams. No way to have a proper hearing, puns take language to the point of unintelligibility. A crack-up.

Communication breakdown. In **Weight and See,** for instance, when "your fortune told while you weigh." Only the fortuitous convergence in the word mattering. Or in **Lost and Found,** another accident. Gumby: "Have you seen my coin?" Mr. Backwards: "You bet!" Coining a phrase to expose lingo as a chance meeting.

Take King Ott listening to his son Harold. The kid wants to give his true love "something special" for Christmas. Ott thinks especially cheap. "The best thing you can give her is a partridge in a pear tree. It's very proper and very inexpensive. They are on sale right now at discount prices." Minting two meanings in one.

Gumby and friends make sense slide with slick slang. They speak an English that re-expresses idioms. Take the Blockhead's ripoff tactics in **Even Steven.** "Highway robbery, I call it." Right on the button. Gumbasian puns describe actions in spite of themselves. Other car colloquialisms tuned up: in **Motor Mania,** Gumby and Pokey take their buggies for a literal "spin" and give rich racer Reggie "a run

for his money." And in **Gumby League,** more of this same body of material: Kap's catch uses "the old head," Gumby's "the old stomach." A repeated operation that puts speech in stitches.

These clay tongue twisters turn a phrase around just to have it their way. In **The Ferris Wheel Mystery,** the Blockheads get caught "red handed." Correction made for Pokey in a quirky construction: "red ponied." **All Broken Up,** Gumby adds a little extra sound, dis-a-vowels to deafen meaning. "Everything has gong wrong." **Hot Ice:** it's just "jewel bait" for jailed Zveegee. Or Prickle pooh-poohs the **Shady Lemonade** soda jerk with "sour grapes." Goo retorts with some juiced-up jargon of her own. "You mean 'sour lemons.' " A new twist on an old expresssion.

With all these vernacular pranks, Gumby dialogue can easily degenerate into pun fests with the masters going head to head. Sparring with words as weapons. *Can You Top This* for the quick-tongued. The game's goal: come up with the worst/best pun, get the biggest laugh, put an abrupt stop to sense. In sum, some nonsense. Goo gets first crack in **El Toro.** "My goodness. That bull was just a big bully!" Prickle's not to be outdone. "Yeah . . . but we got quite a charge out of him!" Going around the horn, glib Gumby tops them all with a double whammy: "Heh, heh. You know, if that little guy hadn't horned in, we'd still be up a tree."

Episodes breaking up with the laughter of the four pals. Punning to make a joke of meaning. Lightening the load, taking off words. And for these punsters, that's the end of the language.

Puppy Talk

A Zen question: does a dog have Buddha nature? Well, naturally, when talking about Gumby's pup Nopey. Though if you put it to the pooch straight out, the answer will probably be a pointed "No!"

Right away, you would think this doggy has behavior problems. He's so stubborn, bulldogged. And he performs such dopey exercises in inanity. Most dogs bury bones to hide their loot for another day, but Nopey just buries them. It's a purposeless activity and preposterously pointless—carried out on a grand scale in prehistoric Dinosaur Bone State Park, with all four friends forced to help shove a super-sized shinbone into a pit. Everyone dog tired after this nonproductive Nopey nonsense.

Another bit of obstinate business. Racing around on his motorized skateboard in **Dog Catchers.** Everyone thinks he's gone astray and in terrible danger. But Nopey's just cruising, taking the would-be saviors on a wild dog chase for some free and easy wandering. **Stuck on Books—** not willing to enter the book, not willing to leave it. A muddle in the middle. Holding a branch in his mouth, not responding to Gumby's and Pokey's prods and queries.

Look at how Nopey treats his school marms and masters—startling them at every turn. No respect at all. Exasperated Madam She finally throws him out on his floppy ear for **Puppy Talk.** And the new kid on the block—who promises he can teach even the toughest dropout—locks Nopey in a room under hot lights

with a language record spinning away. Only trouble is that free-spirited Nopey snuck out the door and left the professor in the doghouse. Safe to assume that school isn't Nopey's doggy bag.

Particularly when you already know that "No!" is the only verbal row to hoe. First you think you can converse with Nopey. "You're not afraid of us, are you pup?" asks Gumby, still trying to make **Puppy Talk.** No, doggy says. But then pup pulls a reverse. "We're gonna be friends, aren't we pup?" No! Gumby thinks a mistake has been made, that the approach is somehow wrong. But this hound never quits confounding things. Never afraid to use double negatives to tie up their language in knots.

And though he ain't nothing but a hound, Nopey feels up to taking a bite out of dogma, out of wanting to know what's what. "This is a shadow," says the language scholar of **Puppy Dog School.** No! "Tree!" No! "Car!" he cries, under the wheels in a hit-and-run. No! "Please say bone!" Nopey makes no bones about burying it. No, no, no! Disposing with description. Little gets left as the world dissolves in a word. "To be or not to be . . ." quotes the **Dopey Nopey** boy with the book. No!

Protecting Nopey from the dog catcher, Gumby pops a perfect, perfectly peculiar question: "You're not the puppy that can only say no, are you?" Answer yes and you're not Nopey. Answer no and you still aren't. So the pooch says something else! No! Not connecting—dogfighting with non sequiturs.

"What can I do for you, Nopey?" asks Prickle the skateboard repairman in **Dog Catchers.** Of course the expected reply. But not by any definition an answer, by any means a meaning. The bone of contention here is up for grabs. Nopey takes speech to its limits till it stumbles over

Gold Rush Gumby. *This hound never quits confounding things.*

itself. Becomes a barking noise, a sound effect. No longer negative—already an affirmation, a cry of pure puppy joy. As he rides into the sunset on his skateboard, listen to the puppy yowl. Doggone. "No," letting go.

The Empty Set

Gumby has joined the empty set. Null and void. Nothing—it's something to contemplate. And at the start of **Toying Around** he assumes a yoga posture. Standing on his head. Staring into space.

Becoming a sect member requires that the adept avoid. Self-denial, self-abnegation. In **Gumby League,** he's willing to undertake a fast ball to the stomach to get opened up. A very hole-y man indeed. A Gumby household tradition: in **Robot Rumpus** Dad plays hole role model in his battle with the mechanical menace. Hit and slit by a winging wrench. When it comes to such encounters, Gumby's roots go deep. Down and dirty. Digging it up for Nopey or "in a gopher hole, Mother." No trouble at all.

Pragmatic Pokey is pretty positive what to make of emptiness: Gumby's full of it. Instead of some Zen meditation, the pony's standing by, standoffish, in **Toying Around.** And when **The Zoops** pop back melonish and the clayboy no longer turns a profit, melancholy sets in. No green stuff registers a big zero in his mind. "You got nothing now!"

For Gumby it's a much stranger relationship. Avoiding where prohibited by law in **The Magic Show.** A doorframe hanging in space and two guards block Gumby's next move. They want to regulate entrance and exit, but straightforward Gumby sidesteps the door and slides around the side.

Cut to a new view—a bridge. Of course the authorities want Gumby kept off, but the clayboy plays a trick, utilizing the ruse of the negative. "Someone crossed the bridge!" he cries. "That's right," says keeper one. *"We don't see them!"* They miss the joke of no place. The fooled flee and free up the bridge. Gumby enters the threshold, walking and whistling. It ends on the bridge, in the middle. Suspended.

A number of Gumby episodes with not much to speak of. Silent, in fact. **Toy Capers, Toying Around, Train Trouble, Tricky Train, Odd Balls, In a Fix.** All toy episodes—featuring the boy fooling around on the floor. An empty way to play where all the use in the world will not drain him. The **Foxy Box**—seemingly empty, but no end to the possibilities. Trains and cars, inexhaustible. Mute diversions. Always more to bite off than the gumboy can chew. And empty, still.

A trap laid bare in the void. Never a positive thing, yet necessary for anything at all. A paradox, a riddle. More like a source of laughter. Like the Pesky Indian tribe getting a chuckle out of Chief No Tooth's cavity after **Gold Rush Gumby** performs his oral operation.

It works just like **The Magic Show.** Offscreen, Pokey is fearful and flipping. A loss of faith in no place. "Gumby, Gumby, where are you?" Gumby spiraling through space, lands in a blank. Where oh where? No matter. Wherever he might be an elusion. Dodging the keepers by straddling the line. All thanks to nothing in particular. The empty place—between everything. The laughing jack-in-the-box opens up—"Anything can happen here."

To Be Continued

When Gumby takes his very first **Moon Trip,** the houses are in motion. The ride

Robot Rumpus. *A very hole-y man indeed. A Gumby household tradition.*

itself is dangerous enough—screaming rockets, a nasty belt of asteroids, Gumby in a cold sweat. Even a crash landing. But the end of the story is positively baffling. Gumby fends for himself at fade-out, uncertain of his future. Sitting on a crater crest, crestfallen. It's one of the open-ended ways that Gumby ventures. In this case—his narrative truncated. Cut off from conclusion. To be continued.

Elsewhere the very same story. Gumby left in the breach: stuck in a crate in **The Groobee,** spun short and chubby in **Of Clay and Critters,** zapped to modern art (for the second time) with **Mystic Magic.**

Other friends too find no rest at story's end. Goo breaks out and into puzzle pieces to finish **All Broken Up. A Hair Raising Adventure** finds Prickle red-horned, with no apparent means of reversing the process. Pokey winds up tree-topping tall in **Chicken Feed.** Kap bloats in **Super Spray,** and the **Golden Iguana** starts to move mountains. No consolation, no consolidation.

The end may loom large but Gumby always manages to beat the finish. Though Gumby should be exhausted by **Tricky Ball,** he doesn't show it. He could grab the ball and make it behave, take a pratfall, or tell a joke. But the gumboy skates off the screen, on to some new field of activity. This floating game hasn't ended. It just went to a universe next door.

A continuing series: **Trapped on the Moon, Magic Show, Goo for Pokey, Toy Joy, Toy Crazy, Dog Catchers, Gumby Business, Tricky Train, Train Trouble.** No desire to end it all. Gumby rides the train, slides again. Or lets it pass, legs wide open. Steering clear of stories that stop for morals, endings that could be starting something. In any event, running on still.

And last but not last, a most peculiar

In a Fix. *A kind of anticlimax, staving off something more polished.*

group of adventures. Gumby stories that, without explanation, tail off. Mysterious flourishes that refuse to finalize. **In a Fix.** Gumby sucked up by a cement mixer, poured out by Pokey. Pokey trapped in turn by the green guy. A tooth-for-a-tooth-type tale that swings wide to sign off. Gumby stained gunpowder color, doing nothing at all, watching two birds climb his dirty bump. A kind of anticlimax, staving off something more polished.

Perhaps **Odd Balls** is even less explainable. After tooting every horn in the toy shop, Gumby again stands around without a thing to do. The balls cuddle up like candy kisses next to his legs, rub against him. And that's it. The balls don't make it back to marble state. No delusions about finishing off, Gumby gets lost. It's a particularly oblique strategy. Open to suggestion. Elliptical, yes, but stubbornly unwilling to close the loop.

Light Lessons

"Thank you for letting me leave my boy with you," says the nice mommy, heading for her shopping while **Gumby Baby Sits.** Gumby tries to get acquainted with the tyke, giving him every chance, but somehow Gumby's out on the step, thrown out of the house. "Now just a minute. Who's baby-sitting who?"

Hot Rod Granny. *A state that isn't added, subtracted, cumulative in any way. Or even located.*

Good question. The little boy doesn't respect Gumby as a figure of authority. After all, why listen to a guy who owns his own home yet acts like a child? Gumby is alternately an adult, the president of his own company, and a clayboy kidding around in the toy shop, following the rules set by his parents. Other times something in between—a teen entrepreneur out to sow a few wild crops with his school learning.

The child meets the sage in the age of Gumby, throwing out with the bathwater any possibility of bringing the kid around. And even if he's enlightened, that's not something he can preach. At the gates of Music Land in **Gumby Concerto,** the keeper calls for a password. What's the answer? Gumby doesn't even think about it. A musical note is transmitted to his mind, out his mouth. He forms an "o" and lets it go. A four-year-old could have done the same.

Do-It-Yourself Gumby. *Popping the big one for the still-wondering: What does the Gumba teach?*

Enlightenment is like that. A surprising occasion beyond certainty. Nothing obtained or attained. A state that can't be studied, like dinosaur homework. That isn't added, subtracted, cumulative in any way. Or even located. In **Lost and Found** it's nothing more than grains of sand slipping away, poured on top of Gumby's green head. Altogether a handful of times, until Gumby is buried and he pulls his coin from the pile.

Other, rougher shock tactics bring with them faster-than-light illumination. **In a Fix**—the cannon explosion. **Little Lost Pony**—the smack of a yellow ball. For heavy-duty head effects, there's Gumby walking into a post in **Toy Capers** and catapulting through the roof in **Odd Balls.** In **Little Lost Pony,** Gumby removes the ball from his brain, frowns, scratches his head, ponders, sighs, and starts to smile. Enlightenment breaking down its subject at hand.

At first **Weight and See** foretells something definite. A swami—"a smart guy who knows all the answers." "Will I be rich?" Gumby asks. Sooner than you think, comes the reply, and Gumby immediately stumbles on a small fortune. But further acknowledgments are sent, becoming more indirectly involved. "What will happen to me today?" Pokey wants to know. "You will bump into an old friend." Looks promising. Until Pokey and Prickle ram smack into each other. What sort of answer is that? A kind of koan—a Zen subtle story that startles. Next question from Prickle: "What's my fortune?" "You will have trouble because of a fall." Keeping both feet on the ground, Prickle's surprised by a flowerpot knocked off the sill above.

Prickle—maybe a blooming idiot, maybe a budding Buddha genius. By now a familiar situation in this search for enlightenment. Posed by a machine run by a little man inside, yet which can still blow a gasket when this "truth" gets out. Any mechanism that "knows everything" for sure out of the question. Rather a ceaseless practice. Just wait and see. Popping the big one for the still-wondering: what does the Gumba teach?

Gumby Artist

6

Star Performance

Clay is of the earth, but Gumby was formed to be a star. A performer. When the people must choose a President they nominate a guy green to the ways of politics. He may need a quick run through the history books, but the masses trust him for the tour of duty because he's a great actor. A principal prince of players.

Having reached this stage in his career, it's hard for Gumby to get away. Even at the North Pole—where they don't yet know Columbus discovered America—everyone's heard of Gumby. Crashing the party in **Northland Follies,** the clayboy announces himself. "Adler," the walrus says, "we are most fortunate to have as our guest a real television star." And stars, no less, merit special attention all the time. Even when they've been cast to rebuild an igloo. Adler learns to address headliners: "My TV star friends, kindly hurry up with those blocks, will you please?"

When you're a hit, the parts just keep on coming. Hats off to Gumby, who spends a good time in wardrobe fittings. Safari or race helmet, coonskin cap, space suit, old west sheriff's gear—you name it, Gumby's brought it out of the closet. The clayboy never puts his costumes on or removes them. They appear as needed.

A dressed-to-kill character who needs only a bit of encouragement from Gumby is **Ricochet Pete,** a trigger-happy slinger. Gumby can't take him seriously, and Pete proposes a scare contest in Last Chance Canyon. Showing off, Pete builds a bunch of wooden Indians to string along. A

thrilling drama, ending as a real charade when pistol Pete plays puppeteer with Petey and Gumby on either hand. "I bet no other sheriff would think of solving a crime this way," says Pokey. Pete: "This is more fun than shooting up the town."

It seems that all the so-called bad guys ever want is a chance to get on the boards, be a theatergoer. A perfect demonstration: **The Witty Witch** and her comedy revue. For once Gumby doesn't get the joke. As they're pushed into the witch's special playhouse, the green guy suspects "they'll put on a spook show and scare us to death." He should have remembered that everyone's a comedian. Even witches on broomsticks want to get in on the act. "I needed a captive audience. You see, everybody thinks I want to make you afraid. I really want to make you laugh!" A show-biz wiz.

Ricochet Pete. *Coming to a TV set or theater near you.*

The Witty Witch. *Even witches on broomsticks want to get in on the act.*

Only Pokey has problems relating to life in front of the hoof lights. At first it looks like he's giving a fine performance as animal star Buster Bronc, the **Rodeo King.** Prickle prescribes an antidote—smashing the TV so Pokey can't watch Buster's program and hypnotizing him to enter his subconscious. But the dog-and-pony show must go on. Buster-Pokey carries the act all the way to a live rodeo and bucks great cowboy the Argot Kid.

So who's Buster Bronc? No one can say. But as cameras click, Pokey bows out. The practical pacer settles down to a set image, ending the roller coaster. "You know what?" muses Goo. "I think he got stage fright."

Meanwhile, back at the North Pole, another stage struck. "A fellow could spend all his time being a TV guest star up here." Up north. And up above the pit. Gumby and his playmates putting in new appearances. All of them special. Coming to a TV set near you.

Prickly and Stickly

Among Gumby's friends, Prickle is certainly the problem child. Complex—both braggart and introvert. The fat-egoed brat with the low self-image. Intertwined. He'll whine to you about all his troubles with a double edge. "I feel left out," pouts the world's only living dinosaur. "No one ever notices me. I'm nobody. My life is dull. I'm so plain."

It's plain to see that Prickle is a temperamental type in need of recognition, the group prima donna. An artiste who needs special service at the soda shop. A self-proclaimed distinguished detective who can solve any mystery with imagination. A Dizzy Dino–style miniature golfer with a delusion-of-grandeur handicap.

And recognition breeds an even greater need for approval as the fin-back throwback lets it out even more overtly. "Just skill, my man, skill," he crows, puffing up his **Behind the Puff Ball** antics. "I have to answer my fan mail," he notes to Goo in **Prickle's Problem.** Goo strokes him just the right way: "You sure are famous now."

Driven to extravagant acts of extroversion, this dino diva finds it hard not to hold center stage. In **The Magic Flute,** he steals Goo's tooter and reveals his long-windedness. Pursing lips together, he can make bricks leap to his tune. When he and Pokey transfix the ice cream shopkeeper and swing a couple of peppermint cones, Prickle eats it up. Still striking new veins of bravado: "I wonder if we can make that airplane dance!" he fancies. Too bad this coup de grouse doesn't get off the ground.

Too prickly and stickly, his woebegone wisenheimering lets the tortured artist

out. The yellow guy may be crabby, a dino who just can't be satisfied, but it's also part of high hopes and **Wishful Thinking.** "I wished, I wished, I wished, I wished, I wished . . . ," he starts to sing. Gumby, Pokey, and Goo try to finish these fanciful flights, goading Prickle to reveal his birthday surprise. But no. Not tricks nor ghosts nor logic can crack him.

Dreaming a little dream. To the point where everyone thinks you're a crank who takes everything too far. But what do they say when you start to realize your wackiest, most wayward projects? Wishing to the point of forgetting the world outside, ignoring your closest companions. Building a corncrib, nailing your buddies in, and scheming for Farmer John to fill

Point of Honor. *Too prickly and stickly, his woebegone wisenheimering lets the tortured artist out.*

the crib with roots to help them climb out. Oh, it may appear fruitless. But Prickle has just turned up turnips, and who else could have thunk it?

Pop Goes the Easel

Prickle, the romantic idealist, stuck on the myth that art takes smarts. That art is work in need of a genius. As **Mystic Magic** begins, the gang is admiring Dome-baldi's *Nascent Nymph.* The narrator is ecstatic: "What impressions the art gallery can make on the sensitive mind!" Prickle's in particular. A dramatic declaration from an aspiring artist in search of a portrait as a young dinosaur. "Oh, Gumby. Such beauty! Such joy! I've found a new world. I want to be part of it. I need to create. I want to give to the world. I want to be . . . an artist!" His pals boost his morale. But Prickle takes up art as a struggle, speaking self-critically. "I don't have any talent!"

Trash this tale of talent, all this art as trial in error. The Amulet of Dila deals a blow to these ideals. Put into Prickle's hands, it turns whatever he taps into artyfacts. Even the trash cans. With **Mystic Magic,** Prickle is a natural, resculpting claymate and museum piece alike. A roomful of new art in just a minute or two. A touching tale—with no need to get in touch with feelings.

Prickle Turns Artist. Learning how to please with the greatest of ease. A pop art parable. At first it's just the business: Prickle's Box and Crate Company with the Groobee on hand as an assistant. A carpenter applying his trade. Prickle shows Goo how to package a Chinese vase—a Ming-Ding original. Prickle paints a funny face on this thing, dupes the Groobee into doing its duty, and voilà! A crate job. No hands-on experience necessary.

The owners of these new constructions are critical. One finds things nailed too tight, another spots paint and cries disaster. Ancient ruins. A travesty. But Mr. Real, a famous art collector, drops in and finds a real sense of style, rendering a different verdict on the case. "They're magnificent! Masterful painting. Exquisite art. Works of genius." Prickle mediates between these two warring factions. With a minimal contribution, he's at the start of a new career. Everyday art objects almost ready-made.

With **The Glob,** art again spills over into the everyday. Gumby is in his studio, replete with smock, neckerchief, and red beret. A model artist? His manifesto: "Being a sculptor is fun. It's full of surprises." When the Glob takes on a life of its own, the studio can no longer contain the thrill of it all. A chase across the toy shop and into *Western Stories.* Art opening out as adventure—full of risk, excitement, and the unexpected.

Gumby: a life turning into art. No pretensions. Substantial. **Of Clay and Critters:** Gumby packed into a rubber ball, rolled into a box. Rolling into psycho-barrels and coming out peewee. Spinning a hundred different ways until no one need paint your picture. It's collapsing the frameworks. How to determine the difference between Gumby's Groobee creating a cannonball and Prickle's employment of same? It could take a lifetime. A process piece for clayboy and cosmos. For indeterminacy.

Moving Music

Gumby artistry won't stay set in stone. His visions need some airing out. With the sound of music. But a noteworthy echo: sound resounds. **Too Loo**—tired of playing the same old tune. Gumby's two note pals, Too and Loo, have popped out from on record. "We were so dizzy going round and round on that record, and so tired of playing the same song over and over and over, we decided to escape." Notes need space for their variations, so all three are off to Music Land "for some rhythm fun." Sounds great.

But that's only the first movement. Sound moving any body to the beat. Goo's magic flute sets even the table legs dancing. Blow a few bars and there's no holding the handicapped back. Music Land instruments have the power to play their players. Gumby blows into a tuba, blows himself up tubalike in the process. A jumbo Gumby—larger than life. Or try to play the player piano and the keyboard walks away. Gumby tries again. The grand flies up, and Gumby follows. The piano comes down. CRASH! A break dance.

Choreography in **Gumby Concerto**. Intricate visual rhythms attuned to the music. The concerto hits crescendo and swells out of control for a song-and-dance routine that's anything but. Sound strikes and multiple Gumbys boogie-woogie on pianos. A Gumby Berkeley spectacular— a production number that turns about. A chorus line of Gumby pianos! Spins out.

This Gumby music has to be seen to be believed. And it is. Synaesthesia—seeing color when sound stimulated, seeing sound with its visual effects. Not a one-to-one correspondence between note and shape, tone and color. Rearranging our common senses of sound and vision. Some same-time sensation.

The story of the soft-shelled **Outcast Marbles** in a nutshell. Sound revising the seen. "Every sound would make them change size, shape, and even color." It doesn't take much to get it going—just a beautiful noise. Tipping over the toy boxes. An avalanche of crashing and banging that hits the frequency to turn Gumby's new friends back to marbles. **All Broken Up**—

Gumby Concerto. *No hands-on experience necessary.*

Gumby Concerto. *All three are off to Music Land for some rhythm fun. Sounds great.*

Prickle on percussion complete with bells, gongs, cymbals, and drums. Goo playing herself. For every sound struck, Goo grooving to the vibes, striking a new pose.

Some **Odd Balls** bounce around to every sound, recast like their outcast cousins. Gumby scavenges the toy shop in search of noisemakers to keep the odd balls visually stimulated. Musical accompaniments: a fire engine siren, toy truck and boat horns, a music box. Never knowing how the sound will affect them. To the point of rapid-fire abstract transformations.

Gumby has broken the sound barrier. A celebration using music to excess. In **Gumby Concerto,** fat little notes appear on the top of the keys of the color organ and Gumby rolls himself into the bouncing ball. Making notes, becoming notes. Simultaneity—in sound, insight.

Double Trouble

When it comes to copying, Gumby feels right at home. Maybe that's why the clayboy has such a good rapport with art. A commonsense convention: art designed to imitate life. A process of duplication, a double play. Give it a second look.

The Blockheads think they've mastered the art of doubling. In **Bully for Gumby,** they contrive a mechanical bull to do their dirty work. Wind it up and watch it scare away the clay gang. But when the bull runs itself out, Gumby finds the key to this game, spots the device. It's a crank. Have no fear. "That's just a fake, windup bull!" So he fights art with craft. Double for double. Mock up a big baboon and make monkeys out of the Blockheads. Beat them at their own bluff.

Wait a second. There's something funny about these doubles. They're supposed to be "fakes," replicas of the real. But somehow they've begun to take charge of the action, running the lives of Gumby and Blockheads alike. A repeat performance to sock the Blockheads in **Sticky Pokey.** Pokey's puckered out from G and J's pursuit, so Kap comes up with a copycat to trap them. A hobbyhorse—a model painted

Mirrorland. *Where doubles come first.*

with glue to stick it to them. Gumby admires the artifice. "Pokey, that wooden horse looks just like you." Pokey's eyes have reason to bug out. Pokey staring down the poser: "It's scary!"

An elaborate chase scene follows with the splitting image in the lead, taking the reins. Pokey ducks into the bushes, turns to his double. "Ready or not, horse, it's up to you now." The Blockheads fall for it, stuck on the spot. The realist owes his life to art. "It's probably the first time a horse is grateful to a gluepot."

Meanwhile, Gumby doubles in **Mirrorland.** Looking at the mirror, catching his reflection, stepping through the glass to meet it. But a double doesn't come in just one size. A circus of mirror effects. Mirror lands. A catalog of doubles: long and lean Gumby, fat and stocky Gumby, upsidedown Gumby. Gumby getting too caught up in his own reflections. In fact, mirroring his doubles. To meet them he must meet their specifications, match their dimensions. Identical copies down to a bump flip-flopped.

Doubles dominate his life. They're supposed to be helping him find his coin, but don't count on it. Doubles don't always tell the truth. One promises to tell him, then makes him guess. Another equivocates with a maybe so. Duping doubles. Mr. Backwards is an especially dangerous supplement. First off, he forces Gumby to do everything in reverse—"even talking." Later on, the stranger takes Gumby for a daredevil drive through Mirrorland. By journey's end, Gumby is all stretched out and rolled into a tire. Retired by the replica.

Mirrorland—where doubles come first. From the very first frame: an inverted title read as reflected. Then Gumby skates by, adds in the real thing, stands behind it. Spells it out right side up. In the beginning, the mirror image. Life: starting out from reflection. And art doubled over.

Thumb-Things Up

Pull up a seat in Gumby's living room. Look around the walls and eye what the green guy spies. Get the picture? Well, Gumby's into the abstract. Just over his right shoulder, above his favorite easy chair, you might note a landscape. But mostly Gumby avoids that representational stuff—so you can't see the forest or the trees.

When he's tired of still life Gumby lets loose with a volley of tube shapes, balls with eyeballs, flat pads of clay, sticks of wood constructions. Undoubtedly an assemblage. Shapes you can't just shout about, identify as a turnip or a trout. It's like . . . well . . . it's just "runcible." *What?* A word without a definition. Enunciating

All Broken Up. *Try to shove art under the rug and see the mess it makes all over the floor.*

whimsy. A name for artwork that Gumby's friends and the whole town seem to like— but unlike anything.

The green guy's concepts can't be captured and put in a cage or bound together and stuffed in a box—not even a foxy box. Goo's abstract shape performance turns to rubble when the Blockheads bang a gong. Gumby thinks he can resculpt Goo to her familiar shape with the Sub-Atomic Teleporter, but all he really does is blow the Blockheads to bits and pieces altogether. Try to shove art under the rug and see the mess it makes all over the floor.

Holding plans and patterns are hatched, but the contamination spreads. Though Prickle tries to undo the jaw-dropping, awe-inspiring activity of **The Mystic Magic** Amulet of Dila, he finds that abstract magic operates beyond the laws of logic. One second you think you've stopped it all— turned the security guard back to a security guard, the wastebasket to just that, only that—then you turn around to see Gumby once again subject to gallery humor. As a combine: a huge red foot, a spiral, checkerboards, and a giant eyeball in the middle. But what's the point in going on, detailing the descriptions? Gumby and his pals don't mind really. Better to laugh in the face of abstraction. "Here we go again," pops Prickle.

Gumby long ago stopped objecting. In short, his position has changed. Putting a little distance between objects. Enough so that by holding out the thumb he no longer is held subject. Pokey, as expected, still sees the toys and trees. "I wish you'd never got interested in making clay statues," he tells **The Glob** sculptor Gumby. "You don't go out and play and have adventures anymore, Gumby."

The green guy entertains new vistas through abstraction. He knows that a pose which no one knows just goes and goes. Opens up new playgrounds. Reroutes the grounds for play. It's art not grounded in anything, on very muddy ground.

Gumby Bookworm

Gumby's Booked

Look at books—bound. Binding. But raise an oft-quoted phrase: "He can walk into any book." Gumby opens one up and the volume shifts. The clayboy finds an adventure in reading by becoming a bookworm. Literally. Not the type who stays on the shelf stacking up and packing away knowledge. Rather, burrowings in his borrowings. Puncturing holes in book bindings. Worming his way from cover to cover and discovering new worlds.

Doing it for a living. "It's the easiest thing on earth," says Gumby. But not for Nopey. The thick pup is afraid of getting stuck in books in **Stuck on Books.** He's standing scared in front of the tome *Sherwood Forest* and holding back. Nopey fears a hardcover, a container to trap him. Gumby is imperative, citing and reciting this passage: "You can't get stuck in a book!" He pops his head in, steps his foot down and out to show. Still, Nopey won't go, so Pokey pushes. But now doggy stops short—halfway in. Has Gumby been stumped? Nopey's not cooperating, clinging to a branch inside. Gumby sticks it to him to teach a new trick. The hound bounds after the fetch till he's out of bounds. Stuck on books. "Not afraid to go through books anymore?" The dog bites the bookworm's bait. "Nope!" The final passage.

How can the clayboy be so sure of his reading matter? It's in his moves. Sometimes an easy walking gait, or, in line with good bookworm form, Gumby skates. Sliding and gliding, never stopping or sticking. On the move with one foot up on the world.

And skaters like Gumby and Pokey don't just skim these books. They really get into them. Journeys that revise journals. All of their historical escapades, for example, or a return to Roo's royal family where crazy goo-goo-eyed Prince Harold is buying a **Pigeon in a Plum Tree** for his sweetheart's Christmas treat. Pokey wants to help the chump out. "You'll spoil the story!" Gumby says. It's a rerun, all said and done. "Have a little faith in the author of this story." But Pokey exercises some authority of his own and arranges to gild the gift. For the moment, Gumby's out of it: "Now we'll never know how it ended." But it just did. A novel reissue. The readers have become re-writers.

Bookworms can add an inch here or taper a measure there. Every stroll into

Pigeon in a Plum Tree. *Puncturing holes in book bindings.*

The Golden Gosling. *Two separate spaces wriggle into each other.*

a scroll blows it wide open again. In a tale called **Dragon Witch,** Henry goes over the ground of *The Bad Witch.* He grabs the dragon by the tail and rescues the witch, who doesn't seem half bad. Henry reinterprets the story, and when he cuts out he reprints: *The Good Witch.*

With **Outcast Marbles,** Gumby gets into this writing game. This time the book *Outcast Marbles* comes out to meet him. A talking book. "Oh, little clayboy, do you like books? Well, come turn me over and read me." But as he reads he becomes its writer. Gumby incorporated. The marbles pop out of the book, so Gumby plays host and must plot out the story on his turf. And **Outcast Marbles** ends when he puts the marbles back in *Outcast Marbles*—puts down his pen, so to speak.

Bookworms muddling up the place. All

coming and going, eluding the ins and outs. Blurring them. Sometimes a walk through the covers from toy shop to book. Here, the bookworm acts as go-between two spaces. But sometimes the flaps are zapped—no book around. In a walk across the toy shop from the Gumburger stand, Gumby is somehow crossing the Delaware. Or the golden gosling may fly out from Roo's throne room and land at a clayboy picnic. There, two separate spaces wriggle into each other. No closing the books with these texts. Bookends upended. Gumby's booked.

Revolutionary History

Yup. Gumby has read all the books he can get his hands in. He's boned up on American history, annal-yzing all the proper names, dates, places. He has stacks more at his disposal on the presidents, the Revolution, the Pilgrims, and the wild west.

Gumby and Pokey not only take time to leaf through these catalogs, they leap into the fray, doing their best to protect their country and the course of events. To make sure history comes out the way it was. An hysterical history retold. Relending a hand to the Puritans, whose *Mayflower*'s already made it. **Pilgrims on the Rocks.** "I wouldn't want you to miss your landing," Gumby tells them, "because it's already written in the history books." Or abetting George Washington as **Gumby Crosses the Delaware.** Standing before the father of our country, Gumby reassures George, "If I hadn't read my American history, I'd be afraid to cross the Delaware River with you tonight."

Turned back in the hands of time to turn out history in **Son of Liberty.** Gumby and Pokey pop into the book *American Revolution* and wind up poking through General Thomas Gage's grandfather clock, listening in on the plans to march on Lexington and Concord and arrest the rebels. Gage's red-coat guard tears after the boys. Busting out of the book, into the toy shop, pages tearing as they go.

Groobees versus bayonets? The Gumby jeep up against an eighteenth-century cannon? Gumby is faster than a speeding bullet. A blur to those bygone characters as he bypasses this tried and tested story, as this crazed chronicle runs off-course, as the spies fly back to be book marked. Gumby tells Paul Revere he'd very much like to "stick around for the fireworks." But the explosion is over—there's a huge cannonball hole in the cover and the old book will never be the same again.

History turns its pages in good order, yet the two pals can never keep the place.

Son of Liberty. *Turned back in the hands of time to turn out history.*

Unstuck their schtick. Only after Pokey's price is right do the clayboys, Puritans, and Indians settle down to their turkey. And Gumby keeps confusing yesterday and today—bringing his up-to-date firefighting rig to battle the Indians' flaming arrows during **The Seige of Boonesborough.** While back across the Delaware, "Just call me little Eliza Pokey," says the pony pal, stowed away 100 years before Uncle Tom, his cabin, or his book.

Time out of joint. When Gumby and Pokey find **The Pilgrims on the Rocks** they slide-step. Pokey's complaint: "You've got the wrong chapter." Poof! They're down the hatch and backspacing into King James's throne room. Thrown into the dungeon, Gumby, Pokey, and Puritan host John Howard ignore the bars and saunter back to the ship. Everything ship shape in slippery Gumby fashion, but a seam-sick Pokey is sick of having his timing thrown off. "Next time you want to change history, Gumby, do it when I'm not around."

Pokey may not know it, but he's a witness to a revolutionary history where a school book is no different from any Gumby adventure, from his story. All a dabble and dally for study; a play of myth, with memory slips. With every tale fair game for bookworms.

Gumby Crosses the Delaware—a radical reenactment that crosses over. History staying open twenty-four hours a day. Pokey ponders, "I think we'd better keep a British flag at our Gumburger stand, just in case." "What do you mean, Pokey? General Washington won the battle," the green guy replies. "Yeah, but with our help he may not be so lucky next time."

Past imperfect, perfect, time after time.

In the Mix

Even handwritten stories are typed. Typecast as westerns, science fiction, holiday specials, courtly romances, thrillers. But the Gumby library uses a screwy Dewey decimal system. Stacks books up sideways. Leaves piles of misfiles.

These are *Unusual Stories,* as the spine on one of Pokey's favorites says, with more stuff than most reams are made of. Stories recounted and remounted and readily available for refreshing combinations. Gumby loves a mystery as much as anyone, and often reads for pleasure. But the green guy double-crosses the codes—infiltrating to scramble the signals.

Heroes still abound, though these claymate versions offer revisions, heavily remixed. **Dragon Witch** introduces a hybrid Cousin Henry, sporting a cowboy hat and lasso on one hand and knight's armor and

Candidate for President. *A radical reenactment that crosses over.*

Santa Witch. *Claymate versions offer revisions, heavily remixed.*

shield on the other. Rodgy strains to get it straight. "You're either a daffy knight or a daffy cowboy." Henry says, "I'm a little of both." The advantage of swinging both ways, swinging a rope: "Sir Galahad couldn't do this."

But what can this new and improved, bullish and bearish Galahad do? A hero needs proof. A search. A quest. Henry's request: "All I need is a damsel in distress." A tough call because the mixing of genres breeds missions improbable. Here, no normal lady-in-waiting awaits him. The dragon witch has slipped into the book covers.

And **Santa Witch** too jets in on her broom to save the day, subbing for an ailing Santa Claus and laughing all the way.

"This is going to be more fun than Halloween." But making her rounds, Santa Witch adds a little too much seasoning, giving the kiddies more than they expected. When she shows her face to a couple of tots, she receives no hero's welcome. These babes can't handle her cutting up of classes and scram scared.

The plot sickens and thickens to climax, though clay's unusual stories don't really congeal. They ooze through every volume. **The Glob** has Marshal Dillpickle spouting the conventional western script with sci-fi style: "All right, Monster. You're not wanted in this town, so get out of here before I have to shoot you." Bullets don't decide anything as the lawbreaking Glob devours the marshal, then spits him

The Glob. *Gumby's tales of the unexpected.*

out. An ending with no monster destroyed, no sci-fi disasters. Gumby's tales of the unexpected.

Scrooge Loose—Gumby and Pokey as detectives. Evidence that they wear the deerstalker and bowler of Sherlock Holmes and Dr. Watson. First screw-up: Gumby's gaze falls on a copy of Dickens's classic *A Christmas Carol* and he watches Scrooge skulk out from under cover. Holmes and Scrooge? Humbug! "I see something peculiar," notes Gumby. Second: overstepping classified boundaries. Scrooge slips into *Stories of Santa Claus* and starts substituting rocks for toys in Santa's sleigh. Gumby and Pokey finally find Ebenezer, and just when they threaten to straighten things out and meet great

expectations, they twist them. Screw-up three: Gumby turns cowboy, ropes the troublemaker, and pops him into one of Santa's sacks. A mixed bag. "Gumby has confused Sherlock Holmes with Roy Rogers," points out Pokey. And the mess-takes just won't stop. Plots unraveling, uncategorical the imperative. Santa jumps into his sleigh, and before the clayboys can stop him, rides off with Scrooge in tow. Scrooge tied up but still cut loose.

Taking a Poke

Focus on Pokey. A paginated pony who takes exception, who won't chomp this bookworm bait. Horseplay in a negative frame of mind. Pokey: poking and gibing Gumby. A pessimist pony who can't do this and won't believe in that. Pokey: a bit of a slowpoke, several paces back, uttering sarcastic mutterings. Providing a running, galloping commentary, calling the race from the outside position.

Kind of a crank, Pokey complains for the sake of it. He thinks Gumby takes advantage of his good nature in arranging that **Pokey Minds the Baby.** He straightaway tells the green guy to bug off in **The Zoops.** "Wait a minute, Gumby. I've had enough of your weird ideas for today." And he's not above a nasty knock or two. The critic regards regal Ott: "That king was a clown."

Some Pokey one-liners: "If you don't find gold soon you'll reach China," Pokey barbs **Gold Rush Gumby.** Ba-doom. Another day, a new tale: "It would take a writer with the name of Dickens to come up with a character named Scrooge." Rim shot. And the hits just keep coming from this horse master of sarcasm who's got too many ironies in the fire. When Gumby sets his sights on **Hidden Valley,** hear Pokey under his breath, "I don't see how we can find Hidden Valley if no one else ever did." Gumby assures Pokey that the trip will be an elevating experience. "Famous last words," neigh-says the horse, backing off from the globe-trotting. "I'm all for adventure, but this is suicide."

The last word. Pokey has to have it. Either taking the final punch in stories like **A Lovely Bunch of Coconuts** and **Do-It-Yourself Gumby** or stepping away from the action to sum up what's just happened, what lessons have been learned. A champ at stopping stampeding adventures.

Pokey demonstrates devastating control. He's the one Gumby character who can stare straight at the camera, putting himself in another place where Gumby can't be there or hear. An aside, away. He looks right down our nose in **Haunted Hot Dog** to tell us, "Uh-oh, I smell trouble."

What's the story? Pokey thinks it's all black and white. Stories are full of horse-feathers, while he's a real horse of course. In **Rain for Roo**: "I'm getting out of this book. Gumby can take care of himself." Books are nothing but a "good hiding place," says Pokey. Fine for some fun, but count Pokey out.

Someone, though, is keeping a few of the plot twists secret from this critical star. In **Sad King Otto's Daughter,** Pokey takes one look at the magic malleable morph and scowls. "What good is that? You can't even eat it!" Eating his words, Pokey swallows the morph and balloons out, turning into a bouncing ball. The pony goes up with something he can't put down.

And the super-snide cynic really takes a licking in **Rain Spirits.** First he snaps at confused little Hopi. "I didn't know Indians ever got lost." Then he refuses an Indian treat. "No thanks. I prefer grass." Finally, Pokey spits on the spirits. "I don't see any clouds, Gumby . . . Let's go. It's not going to rain." At last, the friendly neighborhood ram sticks his head in, and Pokey's pretty sore. "Uh-oh, I'm seeing things, Gumby. That goat sure hit me hard."

Seeing things? Our little red realist friend? Sounds like he's subscribing to a new sort of bookkeeping. But when Pokey recovers, Gumby better be ready. To butt again but again.

Open the Box

The art of boxing. With cartons, cages, and containers. Handling without care. Unlike skaters, boxers cover all the corners, close the book. In this fold, some heavy-

Sad King Ott's Daughter. *The pony goes up with something he can't put down.*

weights. Doctor Zveegee—the lab-coated, Lugosi-like sinister scientist, a creep who's into keeping. And two singular species, both a bit buggy: the Mason Hornet, laying gold bricks and walling up whatever moves, and the Groobee, a buzzing busybody with a hammer hand that can't wait to build crates and nail the lid shut on others.

Even Gumby is not exempt from this list of containing contenders, but his attempts to capture the Moon Boggles and Richard the Lion don't look too tryin'. Lock Richard in a cage overnight and by next morning he's bolted. Richard: "I decided to look around and go and see the world." You can't confine Richard to the lion's den. He'll go only when he's good and ready to lie down. That's **Lion Around.**

And Gumby loves his **Groobee** bundle of joy, hoping to nab wild animals for zoo-keeping. Open up the cage and sure enough, Groobee hammers home the prey.

The Groobee. *But there is one catch— too many.*

But there is one catch—too many. Showing off at his hero's welcome, Gumby lets Groobee loose. By the time anyone can blow the ultrasonic whistle on him they've all been boarded up, including Gumby. Condemned to such an end. Groobee hits the nail on the head. The hunter gets captured by the game.

Find Zveegee framed up by his own devices—an Automatic Remote Control Livestock Retriever. Programmed for Prickle, this iron-claw cage doesn't deliver, but bags a mailbox. Later, innocent bystander Pokey gets poked into it. The doctor wanted to be a dictator in the worst way. "All I have to do is activate the controls." But the wheeled retriever has a mind of its own and reels Zveegee in. Pokey sorts things out, tattletaling: "This guy, Doctor Zveegee, was trying to catch Prickle, but he got caught himself."

Zveegee sighs a big "Baaah!" but one lockup is not enough for him. The mad doctor is obsessed, knows only one prescription—stop the circulation by circumscription. The hoarder wants Goo's Moon Boggle jewels locked away in his lab vaults. "I will have the finest collection in the world!" But the **Hot Ice** can't keep. These ice-crystal jewels melt in his hands, as liquid assets are liable. Zveegee's save-up scheme foreclosed by flow. When the Doctor rides his retriever to the scene of the crime, he tastes his own medicine. It's into the cooler and behind bars.

While Zveegee discriminates, handling and hiding only special collections, the **Mason Hornet** has a notion to pound up everything in motion, put everything in place. Panic hits Gumbopolis. Fear of the Mason's foundation course—stopping short, encircling, entombing. Goo and Gumby hit the streets, not goldbricking. The Mason's chasing Goo, but the pure transformer pulls a radical reversal with some blue bricks to the head.

The Gumby glide defames enframing. Frame on frame. The boxes topple—beat boxes. And the hornet reforms, bricklayer to ballplayer. No confining to a crate,

a cage, a container of any kind, as all the cartons turn out too fragile. One box cover borders another. In one box is out the other.

Borderlines

Cuddle up close with these Gumby stories and you'll see the green guy is marked as a twin. With Gumby, adventures often come two of a kind. Double trouble **In the Dough** on a **Baker's Tour. Lost and Found** in a **Mirrorland. Lion Around** after a long **Lion Drive.** Gumby leads a double life and proves that two for the price of one is twice the device.

Yet everyone knows there's no such thing as identical twins. Gumby pairs are close as brothers, but, brother, that's as close as you'll get. Things keep standing in the way. Twins, after all, have to leave some space between them. Some room to breathe. To tell their stories—apart. Gumby episode pairs flex their joints to pack their muscle—bordering, hinging, turning, angling, and folding.

Bordering. There's a fine line between being **Toy Crazy** and finding **Toy Joy.** A rail line. A borderline. Both stories find Gumby trying out toys for size, finding a good fit. A brief, repeated passage: driving the car to the crossing, boarding an engine, and roaring away. A connection that straddles the line, a border that does little but track the distance between two bars. Parallel tracks moving in the same direction. Pounded together, but cut by a tie.

Hinging. Borders set on hinges, going around. Around and around in the **Gumby Racer** during the **Racing Game.** In **Gumby Racer,** the clayboy must become a souped-up roadster when the cylinders just won't cycle, while in **Racing Game** his long-suffering engine holds out till the end. Yet how to explain that in both matches it's the clay car that crosses the line—from left to right in one, and right to left in the other. Gumby pulls a 180, a reverse hinging on a car cartwheel.

An episode turning even further, back on itself. At first Gumby is pretty sure that robots equal **Yard Work Made Easy.** As **Easy** ends, Gumby and Pokey are set for some weekend fun while the metal men handle the load. But just around the corner is a **Robot Rumpus,** where all good turns become a bother. Gumby gets all turned around by these approximately opposite scenarios. By the yard companions, the banging double-gangers. Plying the field, turning over the land.

Angling. In three dimensions, at obtuse angles. A **Magic Wand** bends in presenting a **Magic Show.** The show starts: "Gumby, Gumby, where are you?" Gumby already spiraling out. An opening in the middle—in the middle of **Magic Wand.** An opening that grows as the show zig-zags, branches out. A "Y" without an answer or a final coming together. **Magic Wand** and **Magic Show**—not two halves of a whole, the two instead open up holes, between. A new angle on correspondence that won't follow to the letter.

But will still fold it over. **Eager Beavers** and **Tree Trouble.** Two episodes folding on top of each other. Telling nearly identical tales about Benjamin Beaver's big dam—using the very same footage for most of each story. But folds add furrows, and Gumby always has a new wrinkle to offer. **Tree Trouble**—a fable told to Gumby by a wise old owl. **Eager Beavers**—an account told to the audience that includes Gumby as a character.

Foldings retold: two tale-tellings. Stories unfolding—joined but not gathered together. You gather right if you think Gumby's too edgy to read only one book on a subject. He's hanging out at the threshold. The green guy may be paired off but he's never pared down.

Eager Beavers. *Folds add furrows.*

The Episodes

Following Gumby through his body of adventures, giving each segment some special attention. Not in order to plot things out, but to emphasize matters of interest, thought-provoking odds and ends, what to watch for. (All of the episodes were written and directed by Art Clokey, except those written and directed by Ray Peck and Pete Kleinow, which are indicated with an asterisk [*].)

All Broken Up

Some sound analysis of Prickle's musical performance during "Runcible Rhythm." To prepare the concert, Prickle piles up a bunch of decomposed objects. A fragmentary catalog of Prickle's appliances: parts of auto tires, a bedpost ornament, a flashy pan, a faucet, and scads of unidentifiable exotica. A postindustrial scrapheap, twisted and broken into bits and pieces. Remainders, reminders, junk thrown in every space of his musical mobile. Prickle strikes this metal and makes noise—a cling-clanging series of sonic ruptures that hit the head and the gut. He's burrowing into this pile, feeding off it, puncturing the function of the object in question.

Baker's Tour

Gumby and Pokey are learning how to bake with Mr. Dough and Co. While Pokey may want to cut out, a lesson is being impressed upon the clayboys. In outline form. As the tour moves from room to room, watch out for the passageways. Through the squarish oven door.

On to a red triangle slit, a blue star design. And the machinery operates according to the same absentmindedness. It takes tracing and slicing for sugar and spicing. Cookie cutters—perforated stencils for penciling in the forms. For a cookie cutup like Gumby, it's a self-recognition. Blueprinting the green guy.

Behind the Puff Ball*

Miniature golf: the Gumby game par excellence. A match between close friends Prickle and Pokey drives home the lesson. Notice that the Gumby course knows neither out-of-bounds nor penalty shots. It's all as good as green. An intricate series of rods bar the hole and the volcanic cup. But clayboys love hazards and diversions. Like when puff ball starts rolling off

In the Dough. *It takes tracing and slicing for sugar and spicing.*

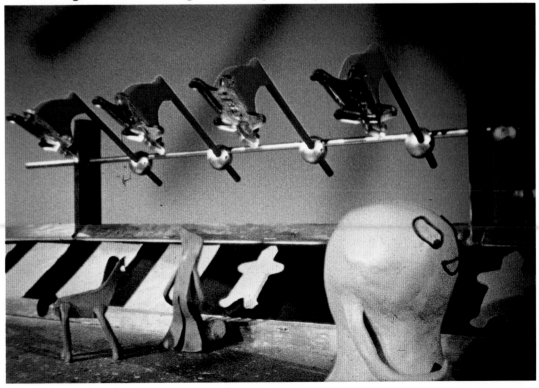

the course and brings the pedestrians into range. The boys play only one miniature hole, but that's enough of an opening.

The Big Eye*

Fuel for thought. Something to consider with confused Pokey. Gumby stares into a microscope, looking for a friend in need. He's a hemoglobin—named Fred—living in the bloodstream, carrying oxygen to all the poor cells. Diving into the action, Gumby finds Fred fighting a someone for a tank and a cart. Who was that? A scientist germ, stealing oxygen. And yet the germs built the tanks for the hemoglobins. Pokey wonders aloud, what does a germ want with oxygen? Well, the germs spotted a giant eye in the sky and are building a rocket ship to explore. But it turns out they've been staring at Gumby's eye. And of course he's now down under the microscope with them. Why make the trip? Stop asking questions. You can't stop **The Big Eye** once it's fired up.

The Black Knight

A chance for Gumby to bail out Roo and royal crybaby Ott from their dark nemesis. Both mounted, Gumby and the Black Knight start to charge. Empty stops between camera shots are super-charged. A screen of bright light. Knight from bottom right, moves cross screen, looking for a fight. Another blank, bright site. Gumby cutting in from stage left, testing his might all the way over and out. Once again in a flash white. Last, a crowd rising from the bottom, scaling the heights. A sequence without fades, dissolves, or splices. Sucking in air. Holding it. Together—with gaps.

Mandala *(an experimental film by Art and Gloria Clokey). You can't stop* **The Big Eye** *once it's fired up.*

The Blockheads

Here's the scene: Gumby and Pokey enter *Western Stories* and try to belly up to the bar. Eight characters animated at once. Cowpokes, brute boozers, a piano player, and even a moosehead all turning purple with laughter. No joints here, all clearly made of clay. And the human—deviant. The bloated pig man: pink belly, pink hands. Smashed red nose, yellow face, sideburns. A piano man with no fingers—just red paws. Black ball head and yellow mouth. And don't forget the shocking green moose. A loose crowd, shaking all over. Rubber babies. Buggy colors.

The Blue Goo

A chase across the skies, with Prickle and Goo tearing after the Black Baron. **The Blue Goo** is a project in projection: casting bodies into the air, seeing shad-

The Blue Goo. *Fixing distances and perspectives, charting trajectories for airships.*

ows appear as pinpoints on the map reliefs below. Fixing distances and perspectives, charting trajectories for airships. Triangulating, shifting. Connecting the dots on the maps, cutting swaths of space with aerial photography. Of course Goo gets her man, but that's hardly the point. After all, it's been such an elevating experience.

A Bone for Nopey*

When Nopey gets bored burying bones in the backyard, Gumby helps the pup move on to bigger and better things. Soon Pokey, Prickle, and Goo are on board. It's the perfect clayboy activity: disposing of the bones of the long since gone, since clay types put coming and going behind them. No place for dead weight or imposing monumentality. Bones are so solid and substantial, keeping a body together, keeping bodies apart. The green guy and

pals make no bones about it. They're spineless, right down to the bone. Make way for the soft cell art of rib-tickling.

Bully for Gumby*

It starts as narrative. Our identification with the clayboys over the stolen apple cart. Then all of a sudden "there's something strange about that bull." Something estranging. A zoom in to the bull's mechanical crank—in five shots. A close-up that fills up the screen. Calling attention to a device—the mechanical crank—through a technical device—the zoom lens. Capacities beyond the power of the naked eye. A filmic factor. Interrupting the flow of a story line. A rupturing effect. Don't forget this film.

Candidate for President. *America needs a stand-up sitting in the White House.*

Candidate for President

Nominated for President by fellow TV star Laddie the dog, Gumby takes it easy. Campaign manager Prickle and Goo find out the secrets of a super chief exec from four past masters on Mount Rushmore. Gumby protests, "I don't know a *thing* about being President." The poll shows otherwise. Their findings—an oar, a pen, an axe, a big stick. Pokey sees schtick: "They look more like props for some comedian in show business." Politics—a joke, a really big show business. Just right for Gumby. The results are in: America needs a stand-up sitting in the White House.

Chicken Feed

Poor Mom and Dad. Their little boy puts them through so much aggravation with mushrooming Tillie. But bringing up Gumby may be a key to why the folks stick together. Consider how very different they are. An interracial couple. Gumbo is red with wigged-out black toupee. Gumba is blue-green in the face with a blond dye job. Both well built, but he's a clay-boy—er, man. Takes after his son that way. Mom has sharper angles, very geometric balls and cones. Finally, Dad is clearly a nudist, but Mom appears repressed. Takes to wearing red blouses, yellow skirts. Very conservative. Maybe opposites attract?

Do-It-Yourself Gumby*

It's hard to transcribe what happens at the keyboard. The clay computer jock sits at the software, punching in a series of commands. But something is lost in the translation. Gumby feeds the machine some letters: m-b-w-f-b-l-c. When digested, it spells "turkey" on the green screen. Other reprograms. G-o-h-p reads out "cage"; h-i-t-i-g-n-p-e-g for a grand "pi-ano." The computer has a mind and language of its own. This magnetic personality voices a running commentary as it produces the consumer's demands. "Kitty cat coming up!" Gives them more than they bargained for. "Roast turkey with all the trimmings. Yum yum." Significant conversions between requests and responses. Signifying—words processing.

Dog Catchers*

A dog race after Nopey in the toy shop. Playthings as a backdrop with Nopey whizzing by. A few of the fun ones merit closer inspection. Two bespeckled fish blown up out of scale. A Humpty-Dumpty with black bow tie looms large. Another monster of a doll with black eye and mop of hair on a tortoise-shell body. A very surreal sense of proportion as these weirdo toys tower over the clayboys. Too many toys to mention, no catching the end of the procession. Enjoy the parade route.

Dopey Nopey*

Economies of scale. Thinking big with a pair of glasses for deep thoughts, thinking small about the gumboy. A minor episode where the camera never moves, where characters stand still. Not even going through the motions. The end of

Robot Rumpus. *Maybe opposites attract?*

the Gumby line in the late 1960s. Talky. Preachy. Talking over a shot of spectacles on the ground. Not much to look at. Watching Pokey stare at something. Reactions to fill the six-minute slot. There's a brief, dizzying scene where Pokey and Nopey crash into a wardrobe for a hint of that old excitement. A clothes call, but nothing doing.

Dragon Daffy*

Prickle faced with an identity crisis. Two extinct possibilities—dragon or dinosaur. In his hour of need he turns to his mom for overprotection. He plays the pampered child and lets Mommy do the talking. Mrs. Prickle is certainly a rare breed. A big-mama type—loud-mouthed, self-righteous. But big-hearted too, and willing to do anything for the love of her little one. When the soda jerk still refuses her boy service, the dinosaur gets sore and throws her weight around. "Don't you talk to my son that way!" Overbearing as it is, **Dragon Daffy** works another side. On Prickle's mother's side.

Dragon Witch

To reach his damsel in distress, Henry has to get through the book *The Bad Witch,* so he turns to the proper page and leaps into the fray. But that's just one readerly response among a host of ways clayboys get into books. In **Rain Spirits,** the happy reading happens by peeping in and popping through the spines. **How Not to Trap Lions** gives Gumby and Pokey a ghost of a chance to get into the African textbook. And **Pigeon in a Plum Tree** features on-its-side entrance. It's the trimensional's multidimensional aesthetic of reception.

Eager Beavers

It's been visible before, this focus on eye-balls. Gumby's big black ones always rolling and shaking. Pokey's fish eyes freaking out of the sockets when given a shock. Even an entire episode called **The Big Eye.** It borders on fetish, and during **Eager Beavers** it's hard not to stare. Wise owl's eyes writhe, hanging from his face. Paper made: both a happy and a sad set. Crumpled down, folded, for emphasis. And see Gumby's unusually active orbs. His red centers straying all over the field. Watch when one starts to cross the eye line. Probably unfastened by fascination.

Dragon Witch. *So he turns to the proper page and leaps into the fray.*

guy finds himself covered with ash. Re-awakened, he's no longer afraid. Empowered to work molten miracles.

Egg Trouble

A two-part episode. First, Gumby saves Trixie's eggs from the other dinosaurs. Second, he takes two eggs to the toy shop for hatching in the kitchen oven. In between: a moment to contemplate. Gumby closes his eyes in the midst of the dinosaur stampede and the screen goes white. All sounds cease, and the sands of time stop as well. Blinking back open, the green

The Eggs and Trixie

Another story of saving Trixie's dinosaur eggs from extinction. Like many other episodes, preceded by a main title of great distinction. Cooking up a multimedia scramble of the visual and the verbal. Two eggs appear. The first breaks into the words "The Eggs." The second crackles and Trixie pops out. Of course: "The Eggs" and Trixie. Then Trixie decomposes to

Egg Trouble. *The green guy finds himself covered with ash.*

Production still. An opportunity to test their mettle.

the letters of her name for the final effect. Trixie: a good egg at the talking pictures. Pretty as a picture or when put in a name. Making a good yoke out of it just the same.

El Toro*

The title animal—bull we've seen before. Featured in **Bully for Gumby** as a mechanical contraption. Here part of a mechanical story. Ticking off a plot that's clockwork: a bull breaks loose from the arena and confronts Gumby and Goo. In a minute they're up a tree. Prickle saunters by, oblivious to trouble. In a minute he's up a tree. Then Pokey trots in to laugh at his friends hanging from the branch. In a minute he's up a tree. **El Toro** does give each of the four friends an opportunity to test their mettle. But their failure produces a wooden series. Giving up without a fight.

Gumby Racer. *Each time reinventing the wheel.*

Even Steven

The Blockheads are back, and Gumby and Pokey have their hands full—of towing fees and two-dollar tacos. But this far in Gumby's long, strange trip, it's peculiar that neither of the clayboys even seems to recognize their arch opponents. Only minutes after the taco fiasco the pony spots them on the road, his memory foggy. "They sure look familiar. I think I've seen them somewhere else." Gumby agrees, but they're caught in G and J's next snare all the same. Mental blocks. Forgetting past encounters—every episode a new relationship with the "thieves," the "bandits." Perhaps it's an active state of erasing. To start again with a clean, square slate. Each time reinventing the wheel. A chip off a new block for rollicking adventure.

The Fantastic Farmer

A passage straight out of Keaton. To get back to earth in *Western Stories,* Gumby has to take flight. On the road, he revolutionizes the transportation industry. Making these incredible connections. He leaves home riding a monorail, hops over to a passing train, catches hold of a fire ladder that swings him over onto a truck, then to a helicopter overhead for extra pickup. For his grand finale, he parachutes for a perfect landing right in front of the book. Circuit maker, breaker, buster.

The Ferris Wheel Mystery*

The clayboys are called in to solve the stuffed-poodle caper. Detect a color scheme. No mystery. Just a question of style. Early Gumby is primary, but this later episode with Peck and Kleinow at the helm has a set preference for pastels. Gumby's office—a pink switchboard with purple-tinted walls. Orange seating on the rides. For toppers, the shocking-pink top hat of Bill Waffle, and the ultraviolet tabletop at the amusement park. Notice these same readjustments gelling during the course of **Behind the Puff Ball,** for instance. The ferris wheel of color.

Foxy Box

In **Foxy Box,** Gumby and each of the surprises stored in the pink safe get a chance to roll into action. Starting up, Gumby grabs a tractor from the box. When it's tracking dirt all over, Gumby flips it over. The wheels start rotating, grinding around. Then a pause and a reverse and another reverse, whirling one more time. Once in the box, the action revolves around a train. Gumby grabs the caboose from behind. The train lunges ahead, whipping its wheels while standing still. The train breaks free and Gumby backspins out of the box, eyes rolling round and round. Everything takes a spin. An extra spin.

Gabby Auntie

". . . Tell me how you're getting along in school, Gumby . . . of course your father was very smart in school . . . why, I remember one time . . . the teacher asked him to prepare a display of milkweed pods for the P.T.A. . . . well, at the time I believe Jennie Farnsworth was chairman . . . and my stars how that woman could talk . . . why, I can recall a story she used to tell about logging days in the north woods . . . and mind you, being raised near that part of the country . . . I can well appreciate her trials and tribulations . . . well, as I said before, I've known many people in the past who have not only been interesting individuals but also . . . show unusual habits . . . why, I had a close friend who kept a flock of rare speckled guinea fowl, the kind that are indigenous to the continent of India . . . and by the way . . ."

G.F.D. (Gumby Fire Department)

Though there are other hair-raising Gumby adventures, **G.F.D.** affords a fine view of hare-brained Professor Kap's gray thatch. Kap's coif flutters before the shutter. As the film advances Kap's cottony wad moves in all directions—assuming a variety of conditions. At first he looks a real bozo, bulging tufts on either side. Then running around flattens it into a stylish pompadour. Still later it's standing straight on

Gabby Auntie. _I can recall a story she used to tell._

The Glob. *Just "for Fun."*

end. Perhaps it's all the smoke in his burning lab that gives him manageability problems. With hairline receding, Kap might appear a rather fringe character. But the professor prefers that windswept look. No permanents. A wave in the breeze.

The Glob

The fun-damental Gumby. His book collection here catalogs the aesthetic of fun. *Draw for Fun.* Another title: *Art for Fun.* This "for Fun." That "for Fun." Even an Ankh book written by Tut: just "for Fun." Fun is: the fact that Gumby, Pokey, and the Glob all start out in the same art studio, yet rush out of three separate books to get to the toy shop. Fun-ky. That Glob won't stay clay and always bounces back—harder to get rid of than fun-gus. That Gumby is a fun-d of information on the joys of being an artist. And that it's almost Marshal Dillpickle's funeral when Glob gobbles him up. Taking fun too far? For Gumby fun's not just a

funny face but anything that's a change of pace. Fun-ctionally unlimited.

The Golden Gosling

Poor King Ott, tied down by his possessions. The story opens with sire sitting in the throne room, counting his 432 golden gosling eggs. The medieval miser gloating over his property. But something smells rotten here, causing the king to miscalculate. The catch is in the hatchings. Egg rolls. Eggs were made to be laid and beaten. Or they crack. After a spell, the golden gosling brings a new chick into the world. Eggs fertilized and disseminated. Not one egg or omelet Ott can call his own. Ott learns to find happiness goosing himself.

The Golden Iguana

A short list of Gumby monstrous behavior. Prickle's pet golden iguana stolen by Blockheads and grown gargantuan by gorging on Kap's Mexican herbs. A chicken with its head cut off—by the clouds. A professor with his super-spray, ballooning the size of his body and brains. Kinda super-freaky. The iguana and his friends are in good form and company. Pokey—the first cross between pony, dog, and clayboy. Prickle—the last dinosaur on earth. Goo—the armless, legless wonder. No wonder the gigantic is something to shoot up for. No problems in proportions. Deforming as a subset of reforming—clay, that is.

Gold Rush Gumby*

Look out for a visual pun put right smack in the middle. Like a filling. In the chief's teepee, Gumby plays dentist, checking out Running Bear's bad tooth decay. "Here, let me have a look." So he bends over and out of the frame. Instead of following the action, the camera is still . . . transfixed. A visual transference performed. It is a chance to have a long look. Stare at the wall. Its design. To gaze at some Indian insignia. Tepee target paintings. Each round like a dart board—a small white circled center, a red mid-groove, and a green outer perimeter. Six white feathers around the dial. The target of attention.

Goo for Pokey

Goo wants Pokey, setting off a series of encounters to snatch him for her own. In class she spitballs him. In the hallways she trips him up. And near the bushes the *femme fatale* makes him eat out of her ice cream. When Pokey visits his doctor to check out whether there have been any problems, Goo lies underneath him as the throw rug. Pokey steps down, and she snaps him up. "I won't let you run away this time," she moans as she tightens her grip. Pokey's caught in her trap, blue-bagged. Goo all over him.

Good Knight Story

Confusion in the kingdom: who's coughing up all that fire? Prickle or a dragon? Easy to guess the answer to that one, but perhaps not the next: how does Art Clokey get all that fire on film? Those bright bursts and shooting sparks that appear whenever something ignites. It's a scratching directly on film. Not too deep—sometimes leaving a trace of blue emulsion. Carving a hundred light patterns—no two the same. Fueling a wavering. Doing the jitterbug. An incendiary activity. Adding layer upon layer of animation while starting from scratch at the surface of Gumby.

Gopher Trouble

It all looks so self-contained. Working way down below the soil, Gumby roots out the gopher's troubles. But, unlikely as it may seem, the gophers have an episode twin. Share a seam with **The Fantastic Farmer.** Where has the cord been cut? After Gumby tries to plow the problems away, for green acres, the crops grow up funny again and a big ear knocks him over into the big black hole. Part of this footage now struck out. The gopher hole covered over, letting the twins go their separate ways. One living above the farm and one below. A perfect operation, excising the incision.

Moon Trip. *Fueling a wavering. Doing the jitterbug. An incendiary activity.*

The Fantastic Farmer. *One living above the farm.*

The Groobee

At the start: a zoo without a lion, a green guy without a plan. Along comes Groobee, who has the hammering bug. One stop on the way: the pet shop, where Gumby is fast talked into his Groobee purchase. He's dealing with a master: W. C. Fields. Running rings around Gumby, acting like an old pal. Patter to put on a big, top show. "Now, my friends, stand back of the cage, and I'll show you what Groobees do." He hawks and barks. The big-nosed caricature in a straw hat inserted in a Gumby story. Drafted from the archives to build some extra texture. Grafted from a little chickadee to a Groobee.

A Groobee Fight*

Gumby arrested for kidnapping on account of his Groobee. A second Groobee on the loose, chasing the clayboys as they search for a whistle that works. The Blockheads behind it all, with a most devious plot. The only way to settle Groobee differences is through a fight, even more unsettling. "I don't think they like each other," says Gumby. A box around one Groobee. Free. Boxing the ears of the other. Free too. A box on a box on a box on a box. A pile-up. To trap a Groobee: build a trapezoid. Gumby's Groobee cuts corners. Crushes corners.

Grub Grabber Gumby*

Mr. Stuff force-feeds Gumby a lesson about overeating. Hallucinating horse as human, Gumby dreams Pokey as kind of a nag. Imagine the pony's head minus mane, ri-bald. Standing upright on a biped's body. Check out Stuff's duds—a snazzy red turtleneck sweater, black pants,

a chef's hat. White-gloved hands with pointing fingers and black-laced footwear replace hoofs and shoes. A scene shot all in red at unusual angles, to further put us on edge. At one point, a full set of teeth gleaming, and evil-streaked laughter abounds. Welcome to a horse of horror.

Gumby Baby Sits*

Gumby baby-sits a big brat. It's a painful experience for the green one. Not many laughs for his task. Things turn so sour that the sound track has to keep reminding Gumby he's performing comedy. A big kettledrum serves as compensation, helps out the routine. Gumby: "I'm going to . . ." Brat: "Don't throw that ball!" BO-INNNG. "Stay in the yard!" BO-INNNG. "Get off the grass!" "Who was that?" Pokey asks Gumby. "The baby!" BO-INNNG. "Let's have it quiet out there or your friends will have to go home!" BO-INNNG. It's a kind of laugh track. Canned. Not exactly a hoot a minute. Gagging through sonic punctuation.

Gumby Business

In which Gumby's upstaged by a pack of understudies. Going about their business, Gumby and Pokey find a gumball machine and Pokey has a chew. But the toy won't work for Gumby. First the gum won't come out, and then the gumballs snake away when Gumby turns his head. He gets up his best gumshoe gumption and enters the contraption. Stuck inside the plastic bubble, it's Pokey to the rescue. The penny machine finally squeezes the green guy out. What a wad. Gumby meets his namesake. Puts into production the first line of Gumby gum.

Gumby Concerto

Taking account of Gumby's split personality. Gumby enters Music Land, plays a tuba and a piano, and suddenly—six Gumbys, different sizes, multicolored keyboards. Twenty-five Gumbys popping in and out, at green, yellow, and pink pianos. One Gumby each for weird whistles with thermometers, cats, and witches affixed. Two at cymbals. Twelve divided from one. A triangle tapping Gumby. Two for sandpaper boards, sticks, and rattles. Gumby striking a file for percussive impact. Two green guys at trombone—one blowing, the other sliding. Thirteen in the great piano dance number. A Gumby at a special color-coded keyboard. And another, a finale. Digital sonic explosions. Some new time signature, fraction. Seventy-four times Gumby.

Gumby Crosses the Delaware

One of Art Clokey's favorite episodes—Gumby and Pokey with George Washington on the eve the Revolutionaries take the plunge. Lots of clever touches, but one prominent dab: the scenes of the river crossing. Dark and vivid blues, majestic magentas and purples. Bathed in the glow of artificial moonlight, the Delaware scenes merit some reflection. Great effects work: Pokey crossing the murky moon river, jumping from ice floe to floe. A constant sheet of sleet streaming in front of the lens. Sometimes dredging Gumby's waters for something deep means no more than seeing what surfaces. What the surface is.

The Gumby League*

It's the big series against the Blockheads and of course the rules of the game are a

The Gumby League. *Where does a baseball belong? Always a catch.*

shambles. Like hands in gloves, baseballs fit in mitts. But once Gumby's team takes the field this league's balls end up everywhere but there. You might call it an error, but with Gumby it's a hit. Follow the bouncing ball down the stretch. First out: the professor takes it above the chin and has a ball rammed down his throat. Second out: breaking through Gumby's body straight into Pokey's mouth. Third out: off Kap's forehead, onto Goo's noggin, tipped into Gumby's stomach cavity. A ball in place of something else, put out in many places. Where does a baseball belong? Always a catch.

Gumby on the Moon

As Gumby takes his lunar leaps, protosynthesizers swell in the background. A swell 1950s science-fiction soundtrack. All the bleeps, gurgles, and squeals of circuits and wires. A typical music for otherwordly activity. Instead of melody and rhythm and harmony—an echoing mass, a cluster of notes that endlessly repeat or defuse but refuse to form tunes. The rules of sci-fi sound—concocting electronic con-

Gumby Racer. *It's on the right track— and the left too.*

ducting that doesn't resemble anything heard on earth. But a musical convention nonetheless. Flipped backward, inverted. A somersault in space.

Gumby Racer

Crafty goings-on during the big rally. Gumby and Pokey are beseiged by Blockhead tricks—boulders on the road, detours, ice cream cones to the head. As the action and engines heat up, the camera too enters overdrive. When Gumby and Pokey maneuver past Jim Snoot, the lens wavers. As the boys close in on G and J, everyone veers wildly from side to side. Blockheads careening to the edges of the frame. Clayboys crossing the line in an attempt to pass. It's on the right track—and the left too. Swinging into action with a hand-held device. Viewers in need of a hand held.

A Hair Raising Adventure

Here an episode that gives a glimpse into the history of style. Hairstyle. Professor Kap, who sees hairy problems every day,

holds a new formula for raising hair. Gumby goes mod. A black Beatles mop adorns his head, hides his bump. The British Invasion hits ultra-hip Gumbasia. The Blockheads too want a piece of the hair action. A more mangy style for them—baldheads to dreadlocks. Roots rockers G and J massaged into the roles of Rasta bandits. Hair-raising Gumby borrowing from the top of the pops.

Haunted Hot Dog*

There's an old expression-ism. Silent. Concerned to the utmost with atmosphere. After Nopey steals a strand of sausages, Gumby, Pokey, and the pup end up trapped in a dark mansion. You notice doors, windows, cabinets—not squared off. Floorboards too not cut to normal specifications. Seen out of perspective. And the deep shadows, the crack of light. In blue and white. The chase after hot dog Nopey has taken a side trip into another dimension. Gumby's face has a stunned expression in the face of all the trappings. This haunted world leaves him reeling.

Hidden Valley

Gumby finally signs on to make a film. The green guy's directing a dinosaur epic, making a picture with creatures supposedly extinct. Pokey doesn't think much of the action, but Gumby feels his film has to be about a Hidden Valley. He counts on this land of the lost. Watching the results, filmgoers the world over count the losses. Mourning most particularly the camera and film—left behind in the rush to avoid the local tyrant. So what makes up this episode called **Hidden Valley**? A shot in the dark: absence makes an art grow founder. Ponder.

Hidden Valley. *Making a picture with creatures supposedly extinct.*

Hot Ice*

Zveegee wants hot ice. The subplot's even hotter. Goo goes princess, playing queen for a day. No longer boring secretary but demanding and domineering. "I'd like to have some attention from my court." The boys held under her thumb, dutifully following her every whim. Gumby dons armor, becomes a knight-errant to defend his lady-in-waiting. And Pokey has to perk up too and bite the bridle and bit. "Sir Pokey, thou will be my favorite steed." She commissions the Moon Boggles to bring her buckets of their ice jewels to adorn her. They obey, even kiss her cheek. Goo sits primping herself in the mirror. Gumbasia's blue angel.

Hot Rod Granny

Pokey's stirred up. Moving at faster speeds than normal, yet voicing no objection. He

Hot Rod Granny. *If he opines here, he'll spoil the teeth-chattering fun.*

ends up riding with Granny by accident. Without glasses, her maneuvers turn increasingly dangerous: forcing cars off the road, wrecklessly paving a way through traffic, racing for a rally, and running from the cops. All the while Pokey sits paralyzed. Even his escape attempt is faint. This pony is usually all talk, but if he opines here he'll spoil the teeth-chattering fun. "Whadya say?" asks Gumby, teasing at story's end. No answer from a horse who knows when not to pad a part.

How Not to Trap Lions

Gumby travels into the book of Africa to hunt the big cats. He has a plan and at first all goes well. The clayboy digs a deep hole, crosses the entrance with bamboo sticks, lays vegetation on top. A classic snare. But then an elephant threatens to overturn their jeep. Gumby and Pokey watch in terror. It's a jungle out there. Already jumpy, the appearance of a real lion sends the boys over the edge, down the chute. Lion looks down, roars. Gumby tilts his head up, groans. The story ends. Midway, with a scare tactic. A stop that leaves the green guy in the lurch. Feeling down. For Gumby, it's gotta be the pits.

In a Fix

A running gag. Two birds that wander into the picture whenever accent the action. Gumby checks out a prop plane and the two of a feather enter. Zipping around, making noise. A second appearance at the cement mixer makes Gumby and Pokey pause. Further grabbing for attention: stealing the stage, the little one jumping the other's back. And later, driving a crane in front of Gumby with the big bird hung upside down. Gumby finishes fixing, and even then the goonie tops him—with another non sequitur. A little something extra for the birds.

In the Dough

Baking in the oven, Gumby and Pokey receive half-baked instruction in the ways of yeast and jelly, rolls and cookies. But this is the way things crumble: "What does it do to the dough?" asks puzzled Pokey, halfway through the tour. "It kneads it," says Mr. Dough. "It needs what?" "It *kneads* the dough," reiterates Dough. "The dough needs the dough?" Pokey cries. Gumby jumps in: "Pokey, he means the machine kneads the dough." "Oh." The friend is still not in on this twice-baked joke, though it's simple enough for the gum one. His needs never change. He needs to knead.

Indian Challenge*

An opposition—making believe that there is a clear-cut choice between fighting and writing, between action and thought. A pale-faced singer of tales, Ferocious Pete: "I can't fight. I'm just an old storyteller. Just a foolish old storyteller." And the Indian myth-maker, Fearless Joe: "I not warrior. I just storyteller." Telling tall

In a Fix. *Another non sequitur.*

tales contra true bravery. Two ways to contest this division. (1) Gumby's solution—a battle of wits, a storytelling contest. When two tribes go to war, debating points to be scored. Acting included. (2) The story undermined *within a story.* Another myth called **Indian Challenge.** Ignore the distinction. After all, this is just make-believe.

Indian Country*

It's a picnic in the country. Preempted. Counting little Indians, the paranoid pack splits. Their green leader remains unmoved. There are no Indians. "You've been watching too much TV," says the Gumby chief. A mega-irony when watching his adventures. How? So many Indian tales—teepee-shaped red men, the ever-popular Peskies, the Plymouth Rockers, the Hopis and their kachina dolls, Daniel Boone's Shawnees (to which Gumby alludes). And what about these scenes where an unsuspecting Gumby drops the Apaches—eyes closed all the while. What Indians? It's that blind spot again. In **Indian Country,** Gumby may have a naïve unknowledge of the plots or a knowing self-mockery. And in between, there's a wide-open space.

Indian Trouble*

The trouble with **Indian Trouble** is that there's trouble with Indians. Indians are usually adventurous friends, precocious

The Siege of Boonesborough. *What Indians? It's that blind spot again.*

Rain for Roo. *The reign of fluids.*

Rain Spirits. *Gumby sees his image in another culture.*

playmates. But here and in **Indian Country,** the Pesky tribe and Gumby turn to stereo types—two sides of an old story that pits primitive Injuns against the great green cowboy. It's so post-Clokey: the Peskies are violent types who must be tamed to make way for civilization—the coming of the mail. Frightening and subduing the "wild tribe" seems to pose no problems for this Gumby. No trouble for the later Gumby scenarists—bent on delivering clichés. And so, stamping out the wild style.

The Kachinas

One of the only episodes where Gumby tags along, plays follow-the-leader. Letting Hopi and the Kachinas raise the storm.

That's because the Kachinas are filling in for him, doing the dirty work. They're rain spirits, the agribusiness gods of Indian myth. Fertility symbols likened unto the clayboy, turning the earth green. Gumby sees his image in another culture. He's devoting some time to gods like Whipper Kachina—an archetype of another mold, with blue hockey face mask, big beak, and feathers. With these creative types at work, Gumby can be assured that Hopi's prayers for procreation will be answered. The green god vegetates.

King for a Day

Roo runs on liquids. Rueful episodes with tears running down Ott's face. A stream of success stories, doing battle with beverages. In **King for a Day,** Gumby gets loaded with grape juice, "medieval soda pop," for spurting sport. **Mysterious Fires**—a hose to wash down the dragon's mouth. Now a little squirt. In **Sad King Ott's Daughter** the elephant does it to the dragon. **Rain for Roo**—showering a muddy red mixture. Once precipitated, a ruin-to-riches story. Roo—blasts from the past during the reign of fluids.

Lion Around
(written with Ralph Rodine)

Richard is a schizo of a lion. Your classic passive-aggressive type. He just can't seem to make up his mind between the responsibilities of freedom and the securities of being zoo-kept. One minute, he's gung-ho for adventure. He comes on so strong that Gumby and Pokey flee up a tree. But before you know it he tames himself, retreating to his cage, into bondage. "I better just stay here in the zoo," he sighs. The split also lies in the title. The aggressive—lion around the world in a day. The passive—just lying around the den. Changes in a lion heart.

Lion Drive
(written with Ralph Rodine)

One of the Gumby greats. You'll never want the story to come to a finish. And it doesn't. Watch this motorist madness stop and go and stop and go. It looks like the end: (1) Gumby, Pokey, and Richard the Lion sit dazed in the aftercrash. (2) But wait. Everyone dusts off for a final joke—Richard drinking all the fountain water before Pokey gets his licks in. (3) Cut to a long coda: watch Gumby go to bed and turn out the light. (4) Still no rest—watch Richard nod off for the night in his cage. (5) Gumby holds up a sign: "The End."

(6) Not the end. Gumby turns the sign over: "Clokey Films." (7) The standard end title. Ending yet again. Over now. Over ended. Given the green light.

Little Lost Pony

A special bulletin about a little lost pony. First there's the picture of Pokey on the screen and then there's the page from *Western Stories* with a missing portion that fits Pokey's specs. Does this first shot fit into the second frame? If so, what's missing? Farmer Glenn and our announcer stand for a narrow, paper-thin view of the book; the pony's picture stands for an absent pony that needs to be brought back. But for Gumby and Pokey—for whom books were made for walking—this picture or that Pokey are always somewhere in between. Traces that don't belong anywhere. So goes Pokey: "I'm not lost. I just decided to look around."

Lost and Found

Mirrorland runs on reversals. Even its car engines. The mirrormobile kicks back. Gumby plays grease monkey, trying to behave seriously. Out come oversized auto parts—a couple of nuts, a gear shaft. A quick inspection and he dumps them back in. In this nutty land, working all the knocks out of the machinery means taking apart. The car rolls reverse with stuff flying out top and bottom. All the nuts bolt, strewn roadside. Knocked up, fixed.

A Lovely Bunch of Coconuts*

A red radio. A close-up to its nameless knobs, clock, and loudspeaker. Imprinted

Making Squares. *Rewrites respinning.*

on the bottom of the receiver—sound waves in delightful patterns and frequencies. The wireless disk jockey is plugging Colonel Dixieman's Wonder Tonic Miracle Growth Stimulator. To enlarge, to amplify, to radiate outward. On to other Gumby stations that rely on reading the audio signals. Flipping the dials around. News of the Mason Hornet comes from out of the box. Reports of the Missile Bird flying through the airwaves on another channel. With Gumby playing the medium. Listening . . . becoming a switching center.

The Magic Flute

Art Clokey never brought up his clayboys to behave perfectly. The four friends alter personality. Characters turned. About face. Encompassing new bearings. Rudderless. Here—as in **Super Spray** and **Behind the Puff Ball**—Pokey and Prickle display malicious roles. Nuisances stealing and assaulting for amusement before they're turned around, turned right. Back to fronts seen before. In **Magic Flute,** the horse and dinosaur are under probation. Not behind bars, like old King

Kong. Just judged as a crime against their states.

The Magic Show
(written with Ralph Rodine)

In Magic Land, Gumby puts on a little show. That turns out to be for no shows. He begins by putting himself on display. Himselves. With his magic wand Gumby duplicates, reduplicates himself into a row of identical green guys which go marching down the line. A troupe of the super-flexing. But this feat of multiplication is just half the performance. Gumby plucks off the doubles one by one till Gumby's gone. And then a voice: "Hey, not me!" A strange moment. It may be heard as a call to identity (not *me*). Or an affirmation of the loss of his ID (*not me*)—permitting him to be Gumby.

The Magic Wand
(written with Ralph Rodine)

"I bet he can do all kinds of tricks." Hocus Pocus that is. But instead, focus for a moment on his magic wand. It's never seen carried to the lemonade stand to sit or stand. But as the magic man leaves, watch for the wand, horizontal to Hocus's left, as he scoops it up. Then watch the nonexistent wand show again—sticking out right before Gumby's and Pokey's eyes. This time with a vertical hold on them. A wand-ering. The new shell game: now you don't see it, now you do.

Making Squares

Making episodes. On a schedule. One hundred thirty times over. Keeping Gumby new, revising and reviving bits and pieces. (1) The train that rides through a dozen episodes. (2) The other toys— rearranged

Gumby Business #1 (never aired). Gumby intersecting Gumby, in and out of the mirror.

configurations, slight nudges for each story to change the scenery. (3) The entire Gumby Gadget Works factory—later re-tooled for **Pokey Minds the Baby.** (4) The joke of substituted heads and bodies, using Pokey and Prickle as guinea pigs in **Making Squares,** and Pokey and Gumby in **Tail Tale.** (5) The theme of reblocking the Blockheads to cylinders rewrites re-spinning to cones in **School for Squares.** Gumbys feeding off themselves.

Mason Hornet*

The hammer. Doing double-jointed duty when dealing with the insect menaces of Gumbasia. One way: The Groobee wields a hammer on his right wing—a tool to box up other animals. Another way: hammers to break up the brick buildings of the Mason Hornet. A public service announce-ment: "In case of attack, a sharp blow from the hammer will cause the bricks to disintegrate." In this case, Gumby strikes left and right, clearing the folks out from the resulting rubble. The hammer: an open-and-shut case.

Mirrorland

You've gotta look sharp when Gumby-watching. Gumby is deeply involved in the search for his gold coin and misses one of the strangest events of the day. Examine the scene closely and spot a big car cruising by, between mirror-thin and mirror-fat Gumby, nearly knocking over green guy. In the front seat—some kind of Gumby in a ten-gallon hat. And the scene repeats itself in this episode's pair, **Lost and Found.** Assaying a busy intersection, Gumby is grazed by a double in a sedan. Gumby intersecting Gumby, in and out of the mirror. Mirror-aculous.

Missile Bird

When the runaway Missile Bird starts terrorizing the citizenry of Gumbopolis, the military bombs away. Pokey sees through the MPs, though, and figures that the Missile Bird is nothing but a hot shot. Missile Bird gravitates in the direction of whatever looks like a bombshell. Getting close to the army's antiballistic device, he notes a similarity that starts his heart throbbing. So Pokey uses a painted wooden bird to lure MB, all stiff and straight and ready to take the bait. A rocket test simulated. A ruse of desire. Taking Missile Bird higher. Getting off on the look-alike.

The Mocking Monkey

The mocking monkey might make fun of everyone—Gumby, Pokey, and even a fierce lion—but it's all in the name of impersonation, or rather im-animalization. Gumby surmises that this monkey is something of a put-on. Turning in spirited renditions of hyenas, elephants, hippos, and

Art Clokey and friends. Alter personality.

flocks of screaming birds. And this mockery carries over, carrying on in the opening titles. In the wrong key—"The Mocking *Wonkey.*" So monkey jumps into the frame and turns over the letter. A little swing, a flip of the wrist. A wonkey imitating a monkey. A "w" acting like an "m." It's the parroting of an ape.

The Moon Boggles*

Two Boggles, loose from the zoo, speak an astonishing, high-pitched language. A little English, some magic words, sound odds and ends, a burp. Deciding what to do: "Whhh, hhh, oooh. Brrp brrp brrp, key, roooff! Ahh, eoooh." Gurgling a circuitous game of hide-and-seek: "Eu-uu. Eeeeee. Breep bo, da—ooom." Gumby and Pokey at a loss for words. Boggles looking out for booby traps that might tumble their tenor, that might trap two figures in search of the figurative. When a Moon Boggle stumbles on a flower, a rose is a rose is a rose.

Moon Madness*

Trouble is afoot. You can smell it a mile away. Cross-country, we're told **Moon Madness** features a bunch of foot freaks getting off on two pairs of limber legs. Pokey and Prickle will do anything to cover up, but Gumby diagnoses pedophobia: "You're afraid of feet." With the shoe on the other foot, obsessive desires and foot fantasies bed in their brains: "You've got feet in your head." The boys need to stand on their own two. Get back in touch with their toes. Maybe a good massage to take off the pressure of the points and enjoy the pursuit of feet.

Moon Trip

A historic step—the first Gumby Adventure. An early green guy with a few personality quirks. If you've seen its relatives, **Gumby on the Moon** and **Trapped on the Moon,** you'd think Gumby's funny walk is gravity-related. He's weighted down or buoying around. No way to stand straight on the lunar surface. But **Moon Trip**'s earthly scenes also keep apace.

Moon Trip. *No way to stand straight on the lunar surface.*

For this one-and-only Gumby, Art Clokey used his toddler daughter as model—miming her side-to-side stroll. **Moon Trip** is Gumby in its infancy.

Motor Mania*

One time it's "punks." Then it's "goofs." Then "bumpkins" and "yokels." Reggie Van Snoot outsnobs the competition as he races Gumby and Pokey to Caboodle Corners. Van Snoot thinks he's in a class by himself—socially superior because of his upturned nose. What Gumby knows is that it's O.K. to be a goof ball. When you don't care about the polished finish on your car, you can develop a cheapskate sort of classy chassis and cross the finish line first. Reggie goes to class in **Motor Mania,** learns a lesson about categorizing, breaking down.

Mysterious Fires

Gumby is going through his morning workout. Aerobics and acrobatics. Gumby working himself over. His version of deep knee bends—stretching, where getting way down makes a tiny green smiling face. For the next routine, Gumby lies on his back. Shaped like a ding dong and practicing his eye rolls. Rotary motions. Finally, from a cube position he's building himself up, adding extra musculature all over his upper body. A shipshape Gumby poses with back turned to the camera. A healthy clay body limbered up and fit for putting out **Mysterious Fires.**

Mystic Magic*

Prickle turns on the Midas charm for everyone he touches. Transforming a statue, garbage chute, security guards, Goo, and even Gumby requires a delicate oscillation of atoms. Their hearts go all a-flutter.

Point of Honor. *You can develop a cheapskate sort of classy chassis.*

Goo, for example, bleeps back and forth four times before her dewdrop body settles into a more aesthetic form—a pile of blue tusks pointed outward. Gumby flickers, faster then slower five or six times. This Gumby strobe light plays top-speed tricks. Emitting a pulse. Creating a sensation. Prickle's amulet op-erates art. In process and product, "Using that thing is a real art."

Northland Follies

As if Gumby and Pokey or Henry and Rodgy weren't enough, **Northland Follies** introduces yet another dynamic comedy duo. Wellington and Adler are cracking up the Arctic regions on their pilot run. This odd couple are the Gumby and Pokey of the smart set. Both very sophisticated, concerned with pomp and etiquette, proper

Northland Follies. *Bantering familiar.*

enunciation. But separated in parts. Wellington plays the effusive, well-meaning walrus, while Adler—a Rodgy look-alike—is a bit of a snob. a snide cynic with all the mannerisms. Comic complements—the sweet naïf and the bitter ironist interacting. Bantering familiar.

Odd Balls

Something old. Something renewed. Something sometimes borrowed. Something red. Take a guess. It's a fire engine. A close second to trains in Gumby's heart, with both Dad and Gumby heading their own brigades. But while locomotives just keep doing their thing, fire engines do a million things. Like putting out **Mysterious Fires.** Or moving the **Odd Balls** through the firing of a siren. After drinking some **Shady Lemonade,** it's an engine that gets the call to pull kitty cat from a tree. **Trapped on the Moon,** Gumby is saved by the fire truck ladder. In solving the **Ferris Wheel Mystery** a fire engine serves as transportation. A vehicle performing many operations, saving many an episode. By no means a mere conveyance.

Of Clay and Critters*

Sounds off-ly noisily. Tk tk tk tk. Tttsssss. Eeepa eeepa kunk aa aa eeep aa kunk eeep. Eeh-eeh, eeh-eeh, aeh aeh. Wrerumpp. Haup haup haup. Hee-hee-hee. Eeeeip, eeeeip, eeeeip, eeeeip. Baieep baieep baieep. Ruff ruff ruff ruff. Sicitta sicitta. Baump baump. Ruff. Rattattatta. Rattatta. Baump-baump, baump-baump. Omp. Omp. Tttsssss. Hhhhhyhhuuu. Ump omp. Tktktktk. Omp omp. Tchaaa. Caoo, caoo, caoo, caoo caoo. Cickkacuka cickkacikka. Cickickkacick. Ammmammmammaa. Ammmmamma. Amamammma. Wwwowwwoww waaaaaaa. Woooooaw. Ooooowa. Rrrrrrs. Ooouwa. Weeeeeweeeee. Tk tk. Waup waup. Rrrrrrr.

Outcast Marbles

Gumby must find the magic sound to harden his marbles. It's a chancy operation. He spots some boxes, bells at bot-

At work in the Clokey Studio. He must be on and off the set. Part of both the cast and the production crew.

tom. But to get to the bottom he's got to knock the tops off. As luck would have it, he sets off a chain reaction. Rolling and tumbling, boxes in motion. Hammering the toolbox, pick up sticks going down, a row of knights rolling over. Gumby enacts the domino theory. Fortunately he hits the jackpot. It's risky, but you can wager that given the chance, Gumby will blow another throw. Probably.

Piano Rolling Blues*

Everyone's knocking the Bach. Dr. Zveegee, intent on ruining neighbor Paul Plunk's piano, prefers "beautiful silence." And Prickle's on one of his downbeat notes about Gumby's piano-moving business: "I can't even read music." But not Gumby—hanging out in the office, feet up on the desk, and whistling the end theme to Gumby Adventures! How did he learn the tune? He must be on and off the set. Part of both the cast and the production crew. Or somehow having his daily life filmed but already entitled to a happy resolution. A heady responsibility, but Gumby just puckers two lips together.

Pigeon in a Plum Tree

A romance in Roo. Prince Harold, son of Ott, has the hots for a girl in the next town. A gift is the order of the day. An as yet unknown present for appropriate presentation. Both Harold and Gumby agree it must be "something special," but what? Ott thinks it should be a partridge in a pear tree, but Harold never comes close to something so obvious. His final choice—part sucker's luck, part pixie dust—crosses great distances and sees many lands. In the hands of his sweetheart it becomes an obscure object to enchant, to delight.

Pilgrims on the Rocks. *"Why is Thanksgiving such a blast?" asks the slowpoke learner.*

Pilgrims on the Rocks

Gumby and Pokey on holiday, with the green one teaching the meaning of the Pilgrim story. "Why is Thanksgiving such a blast?" asks the slowpoke learner. " 'Cause we have so much to be thankful for." Educational vignettes follow—the Pilgrims' progress. The Puritans couldn't have it their way in England. They were imprisoned. They endured great hardships to cross the Atlantic and found America. "I *now* see what we have to be thankful for," an exhausted Pokey comments. "I'm glad you learned something finally." "I'm thankful I'm not a Pilgrim." The moral of the story is a joke.

Point of Honor

Exhibitionists Gumby and Prickle deliver the lines for an updated medieval drama.

Two old hams: Prickle shoves Gumby out of the way as he attempts to retrieve Goo's fallen kerchief. The Great One complains, trying to restrain, but the overactor in him takes over. He must act to ensure the point of honor. Not to be outdone, Prickle allows "no one to address me in that tone of voice." Pretty soon we're in a toy shop duel. Shakespeare and trains. It's what they call avant-garde theater. Gumby's choo-choo spotlight is trained on the dinosaur. Suddenly this morality play has become a revenge tragedy.

Pokey Express

A stare that sticks out. A routine plot is in the making: Gumby and Pokey becoming letter men. They receive some direction from Mr. Mail: "Go toward Devil's Gorge, turn left at Squaw Rock . . ." Suddenly, something undirected, unstaged, uncoached. Pokey turns right, pokes his head in for a mug shot. Mugging for the man with the camera. Taking up the screen, blurring out the background. Fully frontal—face to face. His expression is the shock of recognition. An abrupt break in the action and then Pokey steps back. Rejoins the express.

Pokey Minds the Baby*

Gumbopolis carries its postal services to extremes. A gift-oriented economy, operating only at the receiving end. Dispensing. Pretty packages, unordered. In this episode, Gumby's precocious nephew Goobalee, given up as long gone, is the door prize—plastic-wrapped and marked special delivery. A very special kind of delivery. Present with no strings attached. Find Prickle's golden iguana in the same class, another correspondent in the foxy box. "How did he?" asks horse-sents. "Beats me!" goes Gumby. Whatever way, Gumby welcomes surprise packages. He's very gifted that way.

Pokey's Price

Standard holiday fare, but a serious mood struck. Thanksgiving for Gumby and Pokey, Pilgrims and Indians. Wheeling and dealing in the food trade. The plot of the story—to barter a square deal for the cornmeal and buy Pokey back in the process. Then a change in tone. In fact, multiple colorations when Pokey tries some of that a-maize-ing Indian stuff. Don't touch your dial, there's nothing wrong with your set. It's just Pokey hitting the peyote button. A sequence of test-patterned tonal arrangements. Red pony, green eyes, yellow eyeballs, blue mane. Green, yellow, gold, red. Green, red, blue, yellow. Yellow, blue, red, green. Ugh! Back to earth—Pokey's tone—and the corn pone.

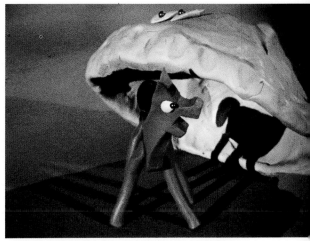

In the Dough. *It's just Pokey hitting the peyote button.*

Prickle Turns Artist*

With the success of his assemblages, constructions for crates and painted vases, Prickle decides to switch media, try his hand at painting alone. But his move to self-portraiture is more complicated. Materially different. He takes an old subject, the representation of the three-dimensional face, but draws it in line with the canvas. The face falls flat—no depth, just a yellow glow radiating outward. Result: a new kind of autobiographical work that no one will want to miss.

Prickle's Problem*

In the midst of watching Dr. Zveegee try to capture Prickle, take a little lesson in photography, on the dynamics of capturing an image with a camera. In his finest hour, Prickle saves a child from the wheels of a large automobile. Newspaper reporters crowd around him for the story, and the cameras go crazy. That afternoon's headline: "Dinosaur Saves Baby." Beneath it, Prickle with the child in his arms. But not a photo. Rather, a rough pencil sketch. Picture this: not something of the mo-

Art Clokey animating a Dinah Shore special. Picture this: not something of the moment, not coverage. Just a piece, a view.

ment, not coverage. Just a piece, a view. But enough flash to set the mad doctor afire.

Puppy Dog School*

Nopey dog in the schoolhouse. A handful of exclamation marks—French, German, Russian, Japanese, English—for the no-it-all pup. Pokey and Professor think the dog picks up something. "He's probably the only puppy that says no in five languages." But no. At the limit of each of these languages—where it becomes a cry and a yap. Like the words on the professor's record, repeated until they become strangers to our ears. Pokey was in the know before the lesson. "He can't even speak one. All he can say is . . ." At which point . . .

Puppy Talk*

As our tale begins, a white Scottie recites a little poetry: "The rrrrain in Spain falls mainly on the plain." Nopey's in trouble. Besides his famous "no" naming, he can't speak a word. Try to teach the puppy dog to talk a thing or two. Speak his own language for the sake of sociability. Nopey, when Madame She threw you out, what was it you no longer had over your head? Roof, roof. Before that moment in your life, how had relations been with your teacher? Ruff. And when you were pounding the pavement, what thoughts and feelings went through your head? Bow wow ow ow ow!

The Racing Game

Put the starting-line scene into slow motion and you'll see a bunch of cameo characters. Big-beaked Jim Snoot, the perilous penguin, commands yellow car number 27. Mocking monkey look-alike Tom Dindy sits next door. His partner gives the crowd a respectful nod. Harry Laughing Itch, a funny-looking fellow given to scratching his chin, drives car number 28. And while it's broadcast that "in car number 66 is Bill Twink," he must be quick as a wink because he's nowhere in sight. They're off and gone in a roar.

Rain for Roo

Gumby's got a big machine for hosing down the clouds—the Dust Generator and Disseminator. Seeding them to stir up some stormy weather and save King Ott's barren land. A scattering of emissions. Condensation and evaporation. Soft and hard core. Liquid, solid, and a gas. No tapping the source of this overflowing reservoir but perhaps diverting it, even confusing the elements when it rains red mud. But that's just more seepage and spillage. Rather than locating one of these substances to oversee the processes or even the point in scattering, Roo dissemination affirms a divided generation in the kingdom. Spills it in advance. Good chance to forget an umbrella.

Gumby Racer. *Gone in a roar.*

Rain Spirits

Pokey gets it in the end. Twice. Punished by Hopi goat Flying Stone for doubting the Rain Spirits' powers, he receives multiple fractures. And in the end titles (which deserve much credit), a visual fragmenting of his body doubles the first rear ending. Goaded again, he spins end over end, his bulk breaking apart, writing out the end. And end footage twice more in **Rain Spirits'** pair **The Kachinas**—Flying Stone throwing Pokey in the swimming hole, and Whipper Kachina whipping the goat's butt. Neither episode upended by the other in end results.

The Reluctant Gargoyles

Another Blockhead caper: tipping over Prickle's high-rise prize, his Tinker Toy architecture. But first a ripe jape. A pie in the face. No, make that a watermelon—aimed straight at Prickle's head. Splat! Prickle turned red-faced. Gumby watermelons aren't content to stay on the vine or even be eaten. They crop up in all the strangest places, like on a train, or in trees, substituting for what Gumby thought would be **A Lovely Bunch of Coconuts.** And they're the seeds that bear magic fruit in the shape of Zoops. Watermelons—those luscious objects that break up logical situations by rolling into view. And splattering their contents.

The Zoops. *They're the seeds that bear magic fruit in the shape of Zoops.*

Ricochet Pete

At first glance you read the title in reference to rootin', tootin' Pete. But he never fires a straying bullet. So bounce it off him and hand the title to Gumby, who deflects old Pete—no longer shooting up the streets. Curtain calling—on the rebound from criminal to playwright. Listen to the ricochets. "You're not gonna scare me," echoes sheriff Gumby, deep in the canyon. But onstage it's Gumby who's forced to skate town. The puppet show carries reverberations, reforms Pistol Pete.

Robot Rumpus

Given a can to cover the Gumba residence, robot house-painters are more interested in line and form. Notice the delicate handling of painterly materials, the vertical brushstroke in the drip tradition. Tag them. Gumbopolis's graffiti artists, with a trash aesthetic. Read the writing on the wall—ROBOT. Mom doesn't seem to appreciate street art, so the robot tries another style. He gives her a whack down the middle. Voilà—body painting! Gumby cleans up, but read the red on the garage door. The robots leave a lasting imprint.

The Rodeo King*

Pokey assumes he's Buster Bronc, the boob tube's rodeo king, and starts bucking up the living room. Prickle plays doctor and pays a house call. What a treat! It's a variation of Gumby pseudo-science. By a few degrees. Atology—the science of that which addles the mind. Pseudofriology—the practice and study of frying brain cells. Sort of. Bycology—a branch of botany dealing with the evolution of clay into plant life. And abbreviated practices: G.O.—Gestalt Orthopedist, G.T.—Gumby Therapist, Ph.F.—Philosophical Sigmund Fraud, M.I.T.—Master in Television. But for all Prickle's credentials—his "advanced hypnocopocus" or his cure for schizites—

the specialist can't break Pokey's station ID.

Sad King Ott's Daughter

Focus on a pun that hits very close to home. Gumby and Pokey hit the concession stands for some serious munching out. Their sweet teeth in seventh heaven. Vending machines for pop, candy, popcorn, ice cream, sugar, chewing gum (of course), and— *morphs?* Gumby the Greek knows "change" is in the meaning, and it's not the kind paid back after purchase. Morphs give you all you want for five cents. But the clayboy has a candy bar

Robot Rumpus. *Voilà—body painting!*

Sad King Ott's Daughter. *Their sweet teeth in seventh heaven.*

craving. Wouldn't you know he can buy only change with his change?

Santa Witch

Santa Witch carries loads of special holiday treats. It's another spirited occasion to visit with the wittiest of witches. A rare opportunity to watch Pokey without Gumby. Plus see a seasonal story that incorporates a one-time-only event. Pokey meanders through the toys. Shoppers are heard overhead, scrounging around. Suddenly a huge hand reaches down to make a grab for our priceless toy pony friend. A miss, of course; nevertheless near and dear. Stop-action animation using people—a

pixilation—referring to such Art Clokey film experiments as *Plucky Plumber* and *Lawn Party.* A hitherto unexplored body of work. Untouched for now.

School for Squares

Even before the Blockheads construct a school for the Indians there's an introductory lesson. In breaking codes. A key punch card is delivered via arrow from the Pesky Indians to the clayboys. Computerized reservations? Gumby expects some data language, but it records in Indian hieroglyph. A puffing picture, a smoke screen. Gumby is befuddled. "What does

Santa Witch. *A different way of seeing.*

it mean?" Indians still speak with forked tongue, so bring in befeathered Pokey to interpret the signals. But as he translates, the puffs recombine. The password is "HELP!" Computer print-out, smoke signals, or even plain English. Just language games.

Scrooge Loose

A different way of seeing. To get a bead on Scrooge, Gumby and Pokey scope things out—using a telescope to be precise. Enlarging on this theme: Gumby has always been able to extend his eye into a spyglass or to swing the thing from behind his back. Dad, too, operates an as-

tronomically large unit in **Trapped on the Moon.** Refocusing investigations note microscopic activity in **The Big Eye, Rain for Roo,** and **Gumby Business.** Gumby is magnifying. Working behind the lens, making a drop of rain look like a meteor. With a slide, upscaling.

Shady Lemonade*

It has to do with a sign: "All You Can Drink for 10 Cents." Two positions stated, lemonade stands. Goo demands drinking to excess for her dime. Meanwhile, the not-so-stupid Soda Jerk knows how to work words for better business. He reiterates, *"That's all* you can drink for ten cents."

One glass only. "Serves him right," Goo remarks as she undercuts the jerk in retaliation. But she can't escape the double standards of language herself. Puns all over the place. Her advert can be interpreted just the same way: two ways. "5 Cents All You Can Drink." **Shady Lemonade**—shades of meaning. Language divided and sliced. Reduced to pulp.

The Siege of Boonesborough

Gumby comes to rescue Daniel Boone and his pioneer borough, saving them from Shawnee Indian attack. The sides seem clear enough until Gumby splits the Boonesborough ranks, peoples the place with scarecrows. They're straw men designed to give Dan more manpower and scare the Shawnees away. But even Daniel Boone is no straight man. "I want the boys and women all to wear men's hats and shirts." A pioneer woman bursts into uncontrollable hysterics at this dragged-out one-liner. Boonesborough's "trick to peace"—a population two-thirds scarecrow, crawling with transvestites. Wonder who's wearing the pants? Taking leave besieged by doubts.

The Small Planets

Seepage in the Clokey Studio: the *Adventures of Gumby* and the animated series produced for the Lutheran Church, *Davey and Goliath*. Slowly but surely, Davey-

The Small Planets. *Gnomic possibilities.*

style puppet animation works its way into the green guy's stories. Meetings between clayboys and boys 'n' girls made of sterner and stronger stuff. The imperious boy on planet one even looks like Davey. Ditto for the girl on the second world—a ringer for Davey's sister, Sally. But in **The Small Planets** it's not just puppets that have invaded, it's an ethos. Gumby resists parental authority—"I'm through being a slave." It's the pentultimate Davey saw: neglecting chores or penetrating deep into the woods against instructions. Perfect for such small planets—gnomic possibilities.

Son of Liberty

So much shooting. Not just due to its length or the stop-action technique. Gumby and Pokey are under fire as they undertake their heroic mission to warn the rebels of the British invasion. A catalog of shots designed to stop them: a bayonet shot straight into the lens, a camera shot the same way that wrecks the Gumby jeep, two rifles ranging right to left that smash the windshield. The film shot through with a violence that punctures. Gumby and Pokey pursued by two armies—redcoats and a camera crew.

Sticky Pokey*

It's another chase scene, cross-country. The wild-bunch Blockheads are riding their motorcycle and looking for trouble. Gang members G and J want Pokey's hide, but they get crossed up by the clayboys. In

Pokey's Price. *The film shot through with a violence that punctures.*

the park, Pokey plays the intersections to his advantage. At one point, he forks them over so well that the B-heads are forced to make the sign of the cross. Silent G and J must be swearing under their breath by now, feeling mighty cross. But they have not yet begun to be double-crossed. The clayboys have planted a sticky Pokey in their path. Down they go, in chains. Acrossted.

Stuck on Books*

A very modern scheme enacted in this adventure. In most of Gumby's textual exploits, the book serves merely as a site for the action to take place, where the plot develops. A locale between the book-ends. Here, Gumby's walk through books becomes an end in itself. The story skeleton steps to the body of the action. Form becomes content. How to get Nopey through the covers and back as the object of their quest. And when Nopey has mastered the machinery (the book's ins and outs), when it's time for something other than self-reference—it's over.

Super Spray*

Condensed form in a clayboy may save material, but Prickle and Pokey both worry over their small-fry status. In need of a shrink and begging Kap for the aerosol antidote. It's a crisis of character. Is little Prickle Prickle still? Is a puny Pokey a pony? For Prickle and Pokey, it's just not the same. When all the air is pricked out, so to speak, the boys get down to something that needs to be reiterated. A super-spray and its repetitions make a world of difference. It's their mist opportunity.

Tail Tale*

Gumby is blinded by the light. Mathematical formulas that double, even triple the speed of sunlight. The flashy light show performed by the Sub-Atomic Teleporter. An orb drawn on a blackboard, made astronomical with orbits. A blue drawing making a funny: the man in the sun, its rays sticking out like tails. **Tail Tale** glitters with such sunlit substitutions. Gumby follows the sun and flies on past light with his teleporter. The sun is responsible, but Gumby will never capture its setting. After all, it takes some distance (just a shade) for the sun to shine, to catch some rays.

This Little Piggy*

When Piggy won't eat, Grandpa has the answer. But who is that masked old man? Behind the mustache, the straw in his mouth, and that "well shucks" manner lies a Gumby—green and bumpy just the same. Grandpa isn't the only relative who's relatively identical. The green guy's gabby Auntie is Gumby in a dress. Dad's the red version, and Goobalee is just shrunk down and pale. Again: who's masquerading as our hero? Not an identity, not a boy hiding behind some whiskers, not indelible. An impressionist.

Too Loo

Too and Loo loose and Sour Note out to arrest their flight. Sour is an enthusiastic pursuer who can make the big leap between objects. A use of the imagination— Sour needs a vehicle, something for air travel, to track down the escapees. A flying saucer might do, but where to find one? He notes the record album. Round. Smooth. Shiny. Seems likely. So he's soon bouncing from the turntable into space, flitting from landing to landing. Transported ever onward. Drawn on in search of the proper notations. Free-fall associating.

Toy Capers

For each toy caper, a charade of sorts. Gumby is clowning around, just jests and gestures. The scratch of the bump, the hand extended to halt, the pose of the thinker, the wipe of the brow. Whew! Getting the point across, only pointing

Too Loo. *Too and Loo loose.*

In the Dough. *Getting the point across, only pointing allowed.*

allowed. Or the chain of reactions on an expressive face. The open mouth of wonder, putting on a happy face, the knitted brow. Yipes! See the silent writing of a master mime. Making another face, a physical flourish. Sure, there's exaggeration here. As usual, Gumby is overextending himself.

Toy Crazy

Gumby makes the toy rounds, choosing his own birthday present. Yet that's only half the story. **Toy Crazy** affords a fantastic glimpse of Gumbasia. In the family's lovely home, the camera faces right. As Gumby somersaults toward us, notice the world outside. It's blank and blue—a completely bare, barely there landscape. Mom walks across the room to the kitchen area and the camera shifts left. Look out the window and note the transposition: bushes, sidewalks, cute little frame homes. The neighborhood has changed. It's a house divided. Gumby resides somewhere between these connected shots, wedged into the continuum. Split-leveled. Splitsville.

Toy Fun

Pokey trails Gumby as he horses around the toy shop floor. Count the close-ups to Pokey looking on open-mouthed in amazement as the clayboy shows off. Pokey plays the passive of the pair, ever watchful, until they reach the kaleidoscope and this stable vision breaks apart. Leaving the spectator in doubt as horse heads shoot out in every direction, in collision. With nothing doing, Pokey's on exhibit. Under the toy's super-vision—Pokey sidelined to every side.

Toying Around

In this toy vignette, special sound effects toy with the viewer's head. At the outset, a boat appears to be at sea, cruising. Sounds of ocean waves and singing sea gulls overhead in this nautical scene. But docked boats block a direct view. Gumby pops up from below deck, hoisting the ship in his hands. This ocean floor was dry. With this gesture, Gumby exposes how sound washes over vision. A turning tidal wave. He winks, supposedly to the sound men who have helped craft the illusion of sea-ing. The inside listening out.

Toy Joy

So many episodes with too many toys. Gumby responds, diffuses his desires. In two places at the same time—like an Indian avatar. Pokey does a double take when Gumby practices with these powers. Gumby appears to be playing the piano. When the camera pans, another Gumby manifests himself, ready to take a train trip. Dissolving himself gives Gumby the freedom to do more things. To be attached to no thing. In short, he has extricated himself from the subject.

Train Trouble

Train Trouble reminds us that the green bookworm can imagine textual encounters of the second dimension as well as of the third. Or combinations of the two. Here, it's with a poster billing a bullfight. An accredited collagist, Gumby likes to borrow whatever is at hand. Attacked by the train, the monteur turns to a matted-down matador for a hand out. He strips off cape and torero hat, which turn 3-D

Eager Beavers. *So many episodes with too many toys.*

automatically and throw off the raging train. When through, Gumby throws the cape back flat. Moves on to his next charge.

Trapped on the Moon

Mom wheels frozen Gumby down a hospital corridor. No more words. Dark shadows. In the treatment room the folks slip their patient into some crazy iron lung. And time stands still. Why doesn't someone do something! Wait. Dad slides a lever. The camera pans. An electric charge wavers between two poles. Look closely and see crude monsters scratched and scrawled all along the walls! **Trapped on the Moon** has hit a fever pitch, but as Gumby thaws out this dream dissolves.

Trapped on the Moon. *Gumby jumps up and races down the corridor, hot to trot.*

No more temperature. Gumby jumps up and races down the corridor, hot to trot.

Treasure for Henry

Captured on a pirate ship, Rodgy and Henry fear it's the end of the line. "Walk the plank, you swine!" orders the captain. Rodgy takes the lead, speaking up. "Bears before birds, buddy!" he tells Henry. Animal cruelty? No. It's just that Rodgy knows his ABCs—alphabetical order. Like the pirates on board—fairly arbitrary. No logic linking the two figures, only letters. "E" before "i." Fragments that follow an absolutely insignificant order, compose a dictionary. But the Captain has made a spelling error. If Henry were a swine, Rodgy would get it first. Birds before swine, smarty.

Tree Trouble

A fable about Benjamin Beaver, his dam building, his inconsiderate behavior toward the animal kingdom, his eventual moral reform—and his anthropomorphism. A grafting of human traits onto animals, instead of letting beavers be very beaverish. Beavers in men's clothing. Engineer outfits to conduct their work. And other human appendages—a pencil, writing paper, drafting table, even proper names. It comes down to a specious disregard for species. These bad-guy beavers stick out among the first year's batch of episodes. They're lumbering through, making do, trapped in a man's world they didn't build.

Tricky Ball*

A simple tricky ball that undergoes basic manipulations. Against horizon, broadened out of proportion. Gumby and Nopey are set in white. No line to mark a floor from a wall. Unlocalizable. Nothing to either side. When the ball drops from Gumby's hand it starts in a straight direction—but not for long. Without perspective the ball can twist every which way loose. Reversing course, confounding a boy and his

Treasure for Henry. *Like the pirates on board—fairly arbitrary.*

Gumby Business. *A chain of train choreography.*

dog's attempts to grab it. It looks like it's caught—held between their legs, bumping back and forth. What's a ball to do? Roll straight back—and up! Out of reach. Out of plane sight.

Tricky Train*

Gumby receives a train mail delivery. A formal exercise in circle and line. A filmed scenario of rail designs. Read the directions and movements. Right to left. Moving counterclockwise, encircling around the Gumby in the middle. Left to right. Approach on a diagonal, back to front. Marching past—left-right, right-left. This time a clockwise patterning. Finishing with a few

flourishes: a loop, a curlycue, a half circle. A chain of train choreography. Figures in a landscape.

Turnip Trap*

Do you recall **Wishful Thinking**? Well, if so, you may suffer from *dèjá vu* during this related adventure that picks up where **Thinking** left off. For the sake of continuity, Prickle's wishing for a wish and Gumby and friends are trying to discover this secret, help make it happen. Prickle does seem to get his just desserts, though his wish gets wishier and washier. At the end of part one, the want has gone out of his head. Over, so to speak. At the start of **Turnip Trap,** the dinosaur's again singing its praises. As for the lapse between the two segments, Pokey says the prickly one "remembered his birthday wish." Or better yet, forgot to remember to forget. Get it? Forget it.

Weight and See*

A very heavy episode. Your destiny predicted by the amazing **Weight and See** machine, designed with mystical symbols— moon, star, spiral. Take a tip and contemplate the spiral in the center that spins around when clayboys step onto the scale of fortune. There's a kink in this slinky's system. It's a pointer with no point to make. What need for a needle on a spiral with no end in sight? The hand of fate works in mysterious ways. Astro-logical. The machine pops a brainspring. A spiral-shaped revelation. As the whirls turn, so the world turns.

Who's What?

An attempt by Art Clokey to start a new trimensional series—a playbill featuring Henry the Bear and Rodgy the claybird. The two went on to further adventures in **Treasure for Henry** and **Dragon Witch,** but this is a distinctly beat version of the pairing. The creation of Rodgy is the birth of the cool. A bopping saxophone slides us through the story. College hipster Henry sports a Harvard sweater and talks like "like I hear strange voices" and like "like what did I do wrong?" "Take it easy there," says Henry. Why get uptight when you're going solo with clay? When you're improvising fusion of Gumby and all that jazz.

Who's What? *Why get uptight when you're going solo with clay.*

Wishful Thinking*

Prickle makes a birthday-cake wish and guards it with his life. He's afraid that telling will spoil all, but when Gumby tries to scare him into telling, he forgets it. Where's the difference? It's just not there.

The former—a longing for something, missing, a wish for fulfillment. The latter—another lack. One projected forward and one long past. To get it out of him Gumby goes ghost. To match these shadowy substances. In the end, Pokey puts the two together: the absence of the future overlaid on an absentminded past. "He wishes he could remember."

The Witty Witch

Pokey quips: "This doesn't make sense." He doesn't know how right he is. One minute, the theater of cruelty—put in chains, expecting the death sentence. The next minute, out of their cage for a form of entertainment—where they're dying for laughter. It's the warp of their perfor-

The Witty Witch. *One minute, the theater of cruelty—put in chains.*

mance artist host, the Witty Witch. Onstage she plays another trick. She's prepared the piano, never knowing how the sound will pound out or pop out. A pie in the face to end the piece. Mixing means in theater, the Witty Witch keeps Gumby guessing. Unprepared for what's happening next.

Yard Work Made Easy

A favorite moment for Art Clokey. Gumby and Pokey truck back to the house with a load of robots—all ready for chores. Before the clayboys can relax, the machines need some refurbishing. Cut to a scene animated by Art: Gumby rolls up to ro-

bot, paint can and brush in hand. Gumby hands him the tools, adjusts the dial on the robot's chest all the way to the left, and steps back. Robot paints a yellow stripe up Gumby's head. Gumby readjusts. Moves the dial right. Robot dumps the bucket on the green guy's head. Turns and blinks. The show-off may displease Gumby, but it's just the mechanics of comedy.

The Zoops

Watermelons turn to Zoops when sprinkled with magic juice. Gumby's jaw goes slack. It what? No clay outlined mouth, no painted expressions stuck and switched

Yard Work Made Easy. *The machines need some refurbishing.*

to match delivery. An Art Clokey experiment—giving Gumby scooped-out chops. A piece of even more complicated animation—repeated only in **Even Steven.** It's a scream. Gumby's newfound hole popping the potion cork. Mouth wide—a lip ledge hanging below a cornered arch—every time disaster hits. Or a slot for soda. Entrance into and out of the body. An orifice connecting the inside with out.

Animating Your Own 3-D Gumby Adventures

9

BY ART CLOKEY

Movies and Puppet Animation

When you see Gumby move on the screen, what you really see every second is *24 separate still pictures*. Each still picture shows Gumby in a position a little different from the previous picture. These 24 pictures are flashed on the screen one after another so fast that your eye is fooled and sees them blended together into one moving picture.

Therefore, all you do to make "moving pictures" is take many separate still pictures with your home movie camera.

To take movies normally, you press your finger on the camera release button and hold it there several seconds while the camera takes 16 or 24 pictures (or frames) each second. But to *animate a Gumby puppet* you merely tap your finger on the release button just long enough to let the camera take only *one* frame. Then you move Gumby a little bit before you take the next frame.

We at Clokey Productions may move Gumby and his friends as many as nine thousand times to make one six-minute-long Gumby episode. It takes quite a bit of time to make a Gumby adventure, but it is a lot of fun to see what you have created if you are careful and move Gumby in an even and natural way.

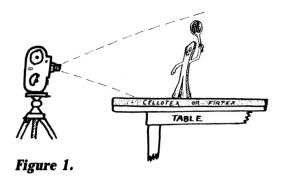

Figure 1.

Things You Will Need

1. 8 or 16 mm movie camera with a single-frame release
2. Lights for your set
3. Gumby Superflex Puppet
4. A flat piece of Cellotex, corrugated cardboard, or Firtex wallboard, ½ to ¾ inch thick, to pin the puppets to
5. Some straight or "T" pins
6. Some modeling clay
7. A head gauge (see Step 4)

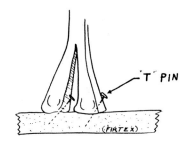

Figure 2.

Procedure

1. Mount the camera very solidly on a tripod so that the camera will not move each time you trip the shutter.
2. Fasten the Cellotex or two or three layers of corrugated cardboard to a table-top securely so that they do not move. This becomes the floor of your "set," and may be painted any color.
3. Fasten Gumby to the Cellotex in his starting position by placing "T" pins through his feet and into the Cellotex (see Figure 1). If he is firmly pinned, you should be able to bend him in different ways without having him fall over. Place the pins on the side away from the camera (see Figure 2), or cover the heads of the pins with a

little bit of modeling clay the same color as Gumby so that they will not show.

If Gumby still seems to fall over too easily, you can strengthen his legs by pushing one or two thin pieces of 16-gauge copper wire or a very long pin up through the bottom of his feet and well into his legs before you fasten him to the Cellotex. Each time you move Gumby to a new position, you must pull out the pins holding him to the Cellotex and pin him down again in the new position. A pair of thin-nosed pliers will help you remove the pins easily.

4. Head gauge. In order for Gumby to move smoothly in your motion picture,

you must move him forward or backward the same distance each time you take the picture. To do this, it will help to make a head gauge out of a 3- or 4-square-inch block of wood and piece of wire (a little thinner than a clothes hanger). Bend one end of the wire into a little loop or circle and fasten it solidly to the top of the wood block with small nails or staples. Then bend the long part of the wire up at an angle, as shown, and the end of it down in a curve so that it holds in the air a little bit above the top of Gumby's head (see Figure 3).

Make a little pencil mark at the top of Gumby's head. By placing the head gauge so that the tip of the wire points down at the pencil mark, you can tell how far you have moved him from where he was. Remember to move him the *same* amount each time. To bring him to a stop after a series of pictures, gradually slow him down, moving him a little less each time for 4 or 5 frames until he is stopped. (This is called "fairing".) Do the same thing in reverse, gradually moving him a little more each time, when you first start a movement. *Don't forget to remove the head gauge before you snap the picture!*

5. How should Gumby move? If Gumby is going to *walk,* moving one leg first and then the other (or slide on one foot, as he does in the TV adventures), you will generally find it best to move him not more than ½ inch per frame. For fast running, 1 inch will do (see Figure 4). If you move him too fast or in different amounts each time, he will jump along unevenly and your movie will be spoiled.

If Gumby is *standing still* facing in one direction and wants to look around in the opposite direction, it should take from 6 to 10 frames, depending on how fast you want him to turn. Remember that it takes 16 frames to make one second of action

Figure 3.

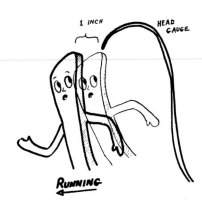

Figure 4.

with an 8 mm camera, so if you want Gumby to stop—to think, or to look at something—you may want to take 20 or 30 pictures of him in one position. The more frames you shoot, the longer he will pause. It is sometimes very important to pause for a few seconds before starting another movement.

If Gumby is *turning around* or *moving very slowly* you can take two pictures of him in each position before moving him to the next position. We call this "double-frame animation." Double-frame shooting

Train Trouble. *For your setting and props, you can make many useful items from miniature toys.*

will help you work faster in shooting a film, but remember: do not use double frames when Gumby is moving more than about ¼ inch at a time, or the animation will not be smooth.

It helps sometimes to take Gumby's place. That is, go through the action yourself. See how you move your arms and legs and head—then make Gumby do the same thing.

By using modeling clay of different colors, you can make other characters for Gumby to play with.

Camera and Lights

You can use sunlight to light your set, but it is better to use artificial lights. If you can, place a light on one side of the camera and another on the other side. Try to make one of these lights about twice as bright as the other.

Since you must take only one picture at a time, your camera must have single-frame exposure. Remember, too, that when taking only one picture, the exposure time is longer, so you need less

The Blue Goo. *To make things fly through the air, suspend them on very thin black thread.*

light. Check the camera instruction book for exposure times. You may have to experiment a bit to find the right exposure for color films.

Other Suggestions

1. For your setting and props, you can make many useful items for miniature toys.

2. Remember to fasten everything firmly to the set, using pins, clay, glue, or tape.

3. Use little wisps of cotton to make smoke for guns, trains, or cannons.

4. To make Gumby's eyes move, take a sharp knife or a single-edge razor blade and carefully slice the red eye pupils off your Gumby puppet. Paint the entire oval of his eye white or light gray, then use little pieces of colored paper for his new eye pupils. You can make it stick with a little Vaseline. This way, you can move Gumby's eyes to make him look around in any direction you choose.

5. To change the shape of Gumby's mouth or eyebrows, use little pieces of yellow paper cut in any shape you wish.

6. You can make other clay characters stand up better if you put thin pieces of copper wire inside the clay.

7. To make things fly through the air, suspend them on very thin black thread. If they are moving fairly fast across the screen, the thread will not show.

We hope you have a lot of fun with your Gumby Superflex Puppet and that your friends enjoy seeing your own Gumby adventures at parties!

GOOD LUCK IN YOUR MOVIEMAKING!

10 Gumby and His Fans

A sampling of Gumby correspondence and appreciation from over the years.

Kids

Dear Gumby & Pokey,

Sorry I couldn't write in green ink because it ran out on me. Is green paper okay? At least my red ink is the color of his eyes! I am in eighth grade, in junior high school. Gumby is very popular there! They draw you on folders, pencils, chalkboards (which get erased by the teacher), and students bring the rubber model of you to school every day.

School is where I first heard of you. What I don't understand is how you are on TV. What I mean is that it really isn't a cartoon, and I was wondering how you move and stuff! Please tell me about that in your next letter. I did write to you before, telling you about how I lost you and then found you, do you remember?

I hope you like the "Gumby's Cello" and the "Pokey's Piano" pictures that I have drawn for you. It took me a *VERY LONG TIME!!* But it was fun. I love to cut and paste things to make cute pictures!!!!!

P.S.: How did you get the idea of Gumby? And Pokey? Ask Art Clokey.

Your biggest fan,
Tina

———————•———————

I always watch *Gumby* reruns. I always wondered how you make Gumby, Pokey, Prickle, Goo, and the Blockheads look so real. I do a lot of ceramics, and things from clay. I made a Gumby and Pokey statue. I entered it in a show and won first place. I even have a small Gumby and a Pokey that you can put into position. I hope you write back.

Your biggest fan,
Rick

———————•———————

I have a rather unusual request. My high school choir loves Gumby and we have taken him as our unofficial mascot. Our choir leader keeps Gumby and Pokey on his piano and we talk about them and use them as an inspiration all the time. It's really a lot of fun. What I would like to know is whether we could get a copy of the music to the "Gumby Theme Song," which I heard at the beginning of the show, just for fun. I am sure everyone in the chorus will appreciate it.

Sincerely yours,
Vicki

———————•———————

A couple of months ago as I was sitting through another endless hour of math class I started thinking about Gumby and how much I liked him, and I started to miss him so I decided to start an informal petition to get him back on TV, and as you can see I have gathered 159 real signatures. No forgeries.

By the way, just in case you wanted to know, I'm a 16-year-old (semi-sane) male and I go to high school. If it's not too much trouble would you please write back to me and tell me if my petition is going to do any good, and in the meantime is there any way, or place I can go, to see at least a couple of episodes?!

Very sincerely yours,
Jerry

———————•———————

A "Letter to the Editor" of an un-identified high-school newspaper.

I have now realized the situation of life in the late 1970s. It is the middle-aged society's goal to eliminate character and instill uniformity.

The school board and all of Rolling Hills' traditional good-guys are embarking on another "clean-up-the-school" project. After all, what would life be without harsh disciplinary procedures? I ask myself where I am each time I walk toward my locker and see three men (Joe Friday, Kojak, and Marshall Dylan [sic]) standing around frowning, looking for another harmless criminal to deal with. Would somebody please tell me if Rolling Hills is supposed to be an institution of knowledge? If I'm here to learn, why is it that the paid employees seem to be more anxious to arrest me than to instill my mind with knowledge?

Tell me, why is it that the people who allocate the money use such little common sense in matters of vandalism? Each time they paint the walls (uniformly) white,

Tina's Pokey. I love to cut and paste things.

they are just begging for some joker to come and inscribe Gumby's memoirs. Personally, I find Gumby far more beautiful than those whitewashed walls. Yet, I realize why those walls are white. Do you? Or has your real character already been erased like Gumby's?

Eno

College Fans

I just wanted to thank you for the fantastic talk and film presentation that you gave on campus! I never realized until I saw all of those Gumby fans how much your work is loved. I also didn't realize that my love for the old Gumby and Pokey cartoons was so universal. If I could do that with anything that I have ever created, I believe that I would attain true happiness.

The Gumby in all of us comes out when I see myself in the child-like caricature of clay—the innocence and trust you con-

veyed is precious. I only wish that today's cartoons could capture that sense . . . if they did, I am sure that they would be as timeless as your films have been.

I hope that the girl from the *Buffalo News* sends you the picture from the paper (of the Gumby sculpture). But if she doesn't, let me know, and I will send you a copy of the one you signed for me. I am glad that you got to see the snow sculpture in person—wasn't that a nice job!!

Anyway, I also think that the other films you showed had a very profound influence on my "eye cells" *and* my brain cells.

Sincerely,
Sarah

Greg S. Taylor, from "A Portrait of the Artist as a Young Gumby," *The Daily of the University of Washington,* April 15, 1983.

My quest for Gumby began last year,

Ricochet Pete. *Looking for another harmless criminal to deal with.*

when something sparked within me the memory of my favorite TV show as a small child. I would sit in front of the set, mesmerized as a green clay-man and his orange horse cavorted across the screen, always ready to embark on some new adventure.

I had my own Gumby, too. A strange conglomeration of wire and green plastic, he provided me with endless enjoyment and helped to shrink the interminable time from one show to the next. His funny green point was a familiar sight in our house, poking out from behind a lamp or out from under the bed. A few quick bends in the right direction and he would sit on my bookshelf for hours or wave unceasingly without altering his cheery yellow smile. He was my friend.

All good things must come to an end, though. One sad and dreary afternoon, my little Gumby took his own life. After a particularly strenuous session of adventurous play, he slit his wrists. It was a gruesome sight. His little wire-bones pushed out through his shiny green skin, just above his tiny thumbs. Fearing that his sharp little wires might also pierce my youthful skin as they had punctured his, my mother threw him away.

———————————•———————————

Charles E. Weigl, from the *Spectrum/ Prodigal Sun,* March 15, 1984.

1966. Christmas. My sister and I hurried downstairs to see what Santa had left us. My mother had dressed us in matching red and white striped pajamas to make the photographs more cute. We stopped in the doorway that led into the living room to survey the situation. Between the tall artificial tree and the black-and-white television console was a large toy chest filled with plastic toys. Embedded

Gumby snow sculpture. If I could do that with anything I have ever created, I believe that I would attain true happiness.

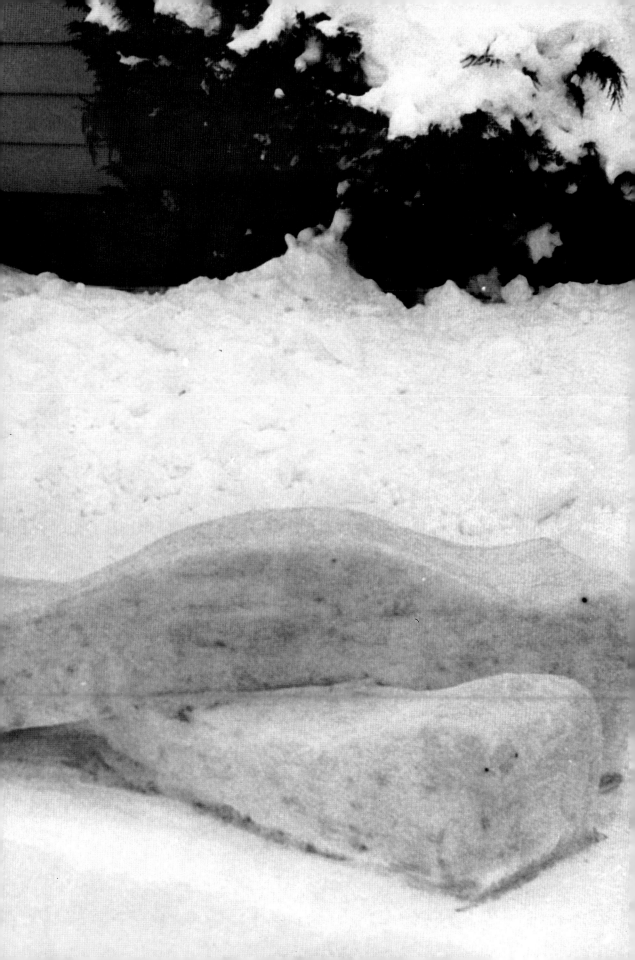

The Siege of Boonesborough. *A large toy chest filled with plastic toys.*

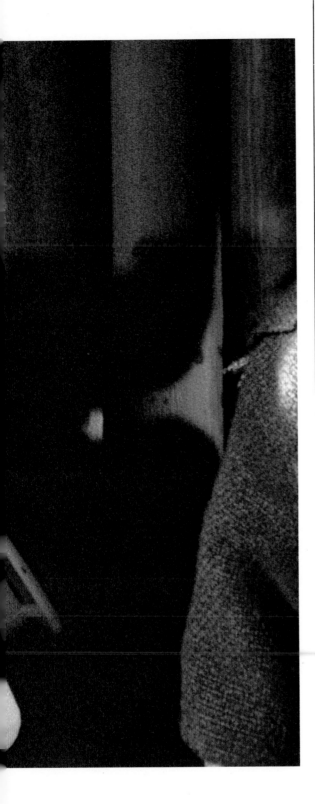

in the pile of gifts, like a flag at Iwo Jima, was a Pokey hobby horse, an orange-and-black head impaled on a broomstick. I knew it was for me, and as my surprised face turned to one of joy, I was blinded by the violent flash of my father's instamatic.

1967. My parents were arguing as they unlocked the door and entered our house, their arms filled with groceries. Something about money. I follow, a two-inch-tall Gumby held tightly in my small hand. The smiling toy had come from one of those bubblegum machines at the super-market. I sat down on the stairs and amused myself by making Gumby jump from step to step. My parents shouted at one another as they put groceries away. I looked down at Gumby and ripped his left arm off. He kept smiling. I inserted the thin green arm in my nose and pushed it up as far as it would go. At some point, my sinuses rebelled against this intrusion with shooting pains. I tried to retrieve Gumby's arm, but it was out of reach. I panicked and screamed for my parents. My nose was bleeding.

Parents

I, too, thank Art (and Gumby & Pokey) for keeping the "child" alive in everyone. That is so important. What good is seri-ousness *all* the time. We all need to laugh, to release feelings, and to love each other. Oh! the beauty and wonder of children. You know, another thing that helps to bring out the simple child is physical activity. Getting really into yoga, ballet, swimming, whatever, balances everything out. Well, dears, keep up the spirit. You have my support and admiration.

Much love,
Shanna

Rain Spirits. *When she opened him, he had a V-shaped cut on one of his legs.*

I received my Gumby—the orange one, because you ran out of green. Gumby made his trip to Vermont to become a new friend to my granddaughter. When she opened him, he had a hole and a V-shaped cut on one of his legs. We had to cut it out so she could not bite it out. I was going to send it back but there was no way getting him away from her. Just wanted you to know about Gumby's foot—if it was to be like that or if it was a defect. Thank you for keeping up the good work.

Marie

About a year and a half ago my two older sons, aged 3 and 2, discovered your animated *Gumby*. Then last winter, after the boys had watched the same episodes over and over again with no less joy than the first time, Gumby was discontinued and replaced by a mediocre cartoon show which was enjoyed by no one.

Just why your *Gumby* was so impressive is not difficult to understand. His adventures were fantastic. As you can see, I too enjoyed the series, and, as a former high school teacher, my tastes are quite decisive where the influencing of young minds is concerned.

After a period of two months had lapsed, I wrote to the station, advising them that Gumby was sorely missed, at least by two children. I received no reply either to that letter or to a second. Just why I am writing to you is uncertain. After all this while I felt sure Gumby would wear off, but it has not. The boys have the Gumby and Pokey figures, but even they do not suffice. Are there any plans for rescheduling the series, and if not, why not? I would appreciate any help you could give us.

Sincerely,
Patricia

The Zoops. *I think it was the trimensional filming effect that made the little fellow stand out.*

Lifetime Fanatics

When I was little I would watch Gumby, and it was interesting because it was not a cartoon and it was not real life. Things in Gumby moved differently and expanded, shrunk, rolled, disappeared—in a very strange way. Gumby seemed like a very powerless hero, who always managed to win out in the end. Gumby gave me the creeps. I would never have wanted to see him walk into my room. Why do you like Gumby so much?

A.C.

When I was very, very young I watched *Gumby*. I thought the stories were pretty unique for the time they were on T.V. It was because of *Gumby* that I became interested in a very highly specialized field of science. That science, however, is paleontology, of which I am sure you are familiar.

The particular episode I am referring to is **The Eggs and Trixie,** which is the one remembered very fondly. I own a video recorder, and recently purchased the hour cassette of Gumby that, much to my surprise, had this episode included. I remember every second of this ditty. But for one problem.

Why, oh why did you put the short version of this episode on the tape instead of the full version?? What happened to the footage of the tyrannosaur stepping on all but one egg, which Gumby takes to an oven and a little triceratops hatches out and chases him? I remember it so well, and I was very sad that you did not use the full version on tape. I wanted to see it in its entirety.

I'm praying and hoping you'll put the rest on another tape. Or is there a way I could pay you to put the other footage on a blank for me? You couldn't imagine what it would mean to me if you would somehow. I would be very grateful.

Thank you,
Richard

I remember my mother buying me the first Gumby flexible figurine around 1963 (when I was about 3 years old). I think it was the trimensional filming effect that made the little fellow stand out from so many hundreds of 2-D cartoon characters all these years. When I think back to my early childhood years, Gumby had a big influence in my childhood fantasies.

Perhaps even too Gumby may be ultimately responsible for my being a cartoonist/artist today. When I think back to my early childhood, back as far as I can remember (1962–63–64; when you're young you haven't a care or worry in the world), watching Gumby at lunchtime while eating a sandwich in my high chair was something special and that specialty has lasted memorably more than 20 years.

I just want to thank you Art for creating more than just a lovable children's character, but an institution that has lasted a lifetime and kept this artist's fantasy imagination alive and well!

Eric

I just wanted to drop you a line to tell you how pleased I am about the revival of Gumby! I remember having a Gumby toy when I was younger and I remember watching the cartoons. One of them impressed my younger brother so much at the time that he tried one of the Gumby stunts at home. He inserted Gumby into the toaster, but to his dismay, Gumby did not come popping back out.

At any rate, I have had a Gumby "collection" which I began before this Gumby revival got going. It started about 9 years ago when I was at a flea market in New York, and I spotted a Gumby in a box of used random toys. He cost ten cents. I was so pleased when I found him, mostly because I had forgotten about him over time, that he immediately elicited a smile in me. That's when it all began. Since then, I have found an old Gumby coloring book, Gumby and Pokey hand puppets, a Gumby electrical drawing set (complete with a Gumby eraserhead), a miniature Gumby from gumball machines and some Gumby action outfits. I also have a few Gumby and Pokey dolls (originals and remakes).

In addition, I had a dream where I was at a store (one of those places that sells old things—collectibles and junk—places I refer to as "stinkshops" due to the various pungent odors they seem to always contain), and I found a version of Gumby that was slightly different. When I looked closer, I realized I had found Gumby's girlfriend—Karbo! She looked just like Gumby except that she had long eyelashes! I've told all my friends about that dream, and now my nickname is Karbo. My husband and I dressed up as Gumby and Karbo for Halloween. I have enclosed a picture of us for your amusement.

Well that's about all for now. Just thought I'd let you know that Gumby still brings pleasure to many, after all these years!

Sincerely,
Linda

Linda as Karbo. She looked just like Gumby except that she had long eyelashes!

Rolling the Credits

The Clokey Studio

Art Clokey
Ray Peck—writer, director, animator
Pete Kleinow—writer, director, animator
Alfonso (Al) Eggleston—art director
Verlyn Larson—art director
Ruth Goodell—story editor, treasurer
Woodword Smith—editor
Colin Young—cameraman, editor
Jim Danforth—animator, puppet maker
Melvin Wood—art director
Bob Danuser—animator, artist
Wady Medawar—lighting, production supervisor
Nick Kurdogla—artist
Roland Shutt—artist, animator, set builder
Jerry Campbell—artist
Ralph Rodine—writer, animator
John Seely—music director
Bud Tolifson—dubbing
Don McIntosh—editor
David Allen—special effects
Harry Walton—animator
Doug Beswick—animator
John Grove—set builder, shop
Bob Kesee—animator
Dallas McKinnon—the voice of Gumby, voices

JOIN THE GUMBY FAN CLUB

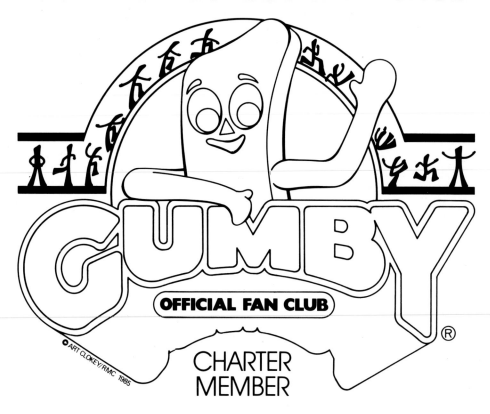

Club package includes a registered membership certificate, newsletters, T-shirt iron-on transfer, and much more "members only" stuff, plus discounts of up to 50% on ORIGINAL Gumby 'n' pals collectors' items! Hurry!

Write to:
GUMBY FAN CLUB
BOX 3905
SCHAUMBURG, IL 60194